PRAISE FOR A MINDFUL LIFE

"To one not inclined to talk about spirituality, Lanna Cairns offers language, understanding of the need for and a way for finding a peaceful space to restore one's soul, repairing it from the damage imposed by the clutter of everyday matter and matters. A gift."
—Andrea C. Alcabes, Executive Director, I.J. & Jeanne Wagner Jewish Community Center, Salt Lake City, Utah

"Insightful and inspiring."
—Natalie Angle, Director, Research Operations & Faculty Recruitment, Huntsman Cancer Institute, Salt Lake City, Utah

"A Mindful Life *is a must read if you are a passionate entrepreneur working towards ambitious achievements. Reading it was like a deep inhale and exhale of grace, validation, and peace. Cairn's reminds us of our own ability to transform, awake, align, and connect with everything around us in healthy ways. You will want to put down your cell phone and read this book."*
—D 'Arcy Benincosa, Owner & Founder of City Style Bar, The Path Workshops, and DB Photography, New York, New York

"A Mindful Life *is an empowering and beautifully written guidebook filled with wisdom and practical suggestions on how to focus one's mind on what really matters. Lanna Cairns gently explains the process of opening to our intuitive inner knowing (Divine Intelligence) and trusting It to reveal our unique purpose for being."*
—Jim Farris, Licensed Practitioner of Religious Science, Heber, Utah

"*Lanna does a masterful job in enlightening us to a greater paradigm; by being truly centered in our personal, business and spiritual lives we can do less and be more whole, joyful, wealthy and vibrant to fully experience the gift of this earthly experience.*"

—Bob Fioretti, Owner of Infinite Possibilities, LLC, Co-author with Stephen Covey, Brian Tracy and Ken Blanchard, Discover Your Inner Strength, Napa Valley, California

"*A Mindful Life is about bringing order and organization to your life thus leading you to a greater experience of peace and comfort in your day-to-day existence, who doesn't need or want that? Lanna Cairns guides you there by beautifully integrating new thought concepts, psychology and spirituality. However, this book is so much more than that. These principles can certainly be applied to helping you achieve whatever you desire in life bringing you to your highest and best self!*"

—Meryll Gobler MA, LMFT, Resource Director Rohlffs Manor, Napa Valley, California

"*In a world that constantly encourages us to seek peace and fulfillment through the outer world of "things", Lanna's message and guidance is a powerful gift. In A Mindful Life, she shows us how to organize our lives by taking control of our minds and helps us to understand why it is so essential to our being to do so. She offers us knowledge and tools to live the life we truly desire, one that nourishes and supports us to be the highest and best expression of our sacred selves. Be prepared to be transformed!*"

—Lynn Holbrook, Mother, Zen Pracitioner, Salt Lake City, Utah

"*Rarely has Spirituality had such a practical application. Lanna Cairns joyfully shares how we can become organized from an inner sense of peace. Her simple steps can have a profound effect in all aspects of our lives. I am deeply*

grateful for the opening to a simpler life with greater peace in my 'being' and my 'doing'."
—Rev. Jay Lang, Minister, Napa Valley Center for Spiritual Living,
Napa Valley, California

"Lanna has created a beautiful, unique, and commonsense approach to and merging of the somewhat esoteric discussion of spirituality and the very tangible one of organization that makes you wonder why it hasn't been done before. With concrete approaches to free oneself from mental and physical chaos and clutter and find spiritual and spatial peace, A Mindful Life *is a must-read in today's frenzied world."*
—Emily McMaster, Designer/Owner - Mabo Clothier,
Salt Lake City, Utah

"Simple, yet profound. Mystical, yet practical. Lanna is masterful at bridging spirituality with everyday realities. This book is a useful and meaningful guide to organize from the inside out and live from the unwavering Truth of your being."
—Rev. Nicole Merges, Spiritual Development Education Director,
Centers for Spiritual Living, Golden, Colorado

"Cairns' recognizes the universal truth that all people carry within them the divine and therefore deserve to live in sacred spaces that renew and nurture us. A Mindful Life *teaches readers how creating sacred spaces in which we live and work supports us in the greater work of repairing the world to be a sacred space for all."*
—Liz Paige, Director of Ethics and Cultures -
The McGillis School, Salt Lake City, Utah

"*Lanna Cairns' new book,* A Mindful Life *will help awaken the body, mind, and senses to develop, change and heal one's life. It offers great tools to clear away confusion, strengthen self-confidence, and develop a positive productive mind.*"

—Gary Quinn, bestselling international author of
The YES Frequency and founder of the Touchstone for
Life Coaching Program Los Angeles, Los Angeles, California

"*It is not hard to ignore these days that our lives have become out of control with our overwhelming schedules. To take the time and effort to organize seems like just another chore to manage and our life continues to spiral into the unending maze of busyness. The key is to be organized, to become more efficient and productive. But how to do so and not loose more time and energy in pursuing this endeavor. Here is an answer…Gleaming from some of the most inspirational leaders of transformation, in* A Mindful Life *Lanna Cairns clearly marries the process of organizing with easy contemplation, creating a relaxed journey rather than a mad rush. This calm path of achieving order consequently produces harmony and a healthier life style each day at a time.*"

—Malka Sabroe-JoHanson, Cabinetry Designer specializing in
Organizational - RC Cabinets & Closets, Sonoma CA

"*Lanna Cairns has radically shifted my attitude toward getting and staying organized. With her clear writing and superb content, she has transformed something seemingly unexciting and difficult into a powerful and rewarding spiritual practice. Lanna includes inspiring quotes, affirmations, and spiritual practices along with practical ideas. This book goes deeper than the usual book on organizing; it is about living a mindful life from the inside out. Thank you, Lanna!*"

—Rev. Dr. Suzi Schadle, Sarasota, Florida

A Mindful Life

Christine, thanks
We did it! for all of your support!
♡ Lanua

A
MINDFUL
LIFE

*A Spiritual Guide to
Making Peace with
Your Mind, Time, and Space*

Lanna Cairns, MA, RScP

AGELOFF
BOOKS

CONTENTS

Preface . . . . *xix*

PART 1: ON EARTH AS IT IS IN HEAVEN 1

CHAPTER ONE: THE POWER OF CHOICE 9

Choosing Success 15

Contemplation: Listen to Your Soul 18

A Positive Way of Life 19

Contemplation: Surround Yourself with Positivity 22

CHAPTER TWO: LAW OF ATTRACTION 23

Vibrational Choice 28

Contemplation: You Are Receiving What You Are Giving . . 30

Mentalization 31

Contemplation: Visualization 34

CHAPTER THREE: FORCE OF GOOD 35

Faith 37

   Contemplation: Quiet Your Mind 39

Transformation 40

   Contemplation: Beginning Something New 43

PART II: YOUR MIND 45

CHAPTER FOUR: UNDERSTANDING CONSCIOUSNESS 51

Beliefs 54

   Contemplation: Believe in Yourself 57

Feelings 58

   Contemplation: Feel the Feeling. 61

CHAPTER FIVE: THOUGHTS ARE THINGS 63

Creativity 65

   Contemplation: Be Open 68

Manifestation 69

   Contemplation: Self-Belief. 72

CHAPTER SIX: LEAN INTO INTUITION 75

Resistance 78

   Contemplation: Trust 81

Acceptance 82

   Contemplation: Inner Stillness 84

PART III: YOUR TIME 87

CHAPTER SEVEN: THE ETERNAL MOMENT. 97

Oneness 100

Contemplation: Transcendence 103

Harmony 104

Contemplation: The Art of Allowing 106

CHAPTER EIGHT: A CONNECTION TO THE PRESENT 107

Guidance 110

Contemplation: Silence 113

Resting 114

Contemplation: Congratulate Yourself 117

CHAPTER NINE: SPIRITUAL TIME MANAGEMENT 119

Slow Down 126

Contemplation: Being in the Flow. 131

Dreams 132

Contemplation: Your Imagination 135

PART IV: YOUR SPACE 137

CHAPTER TEN: VISUAL PEACE 145

The Stress of Stuff 146

Contemplation: The Need for a Refuge 150

Joyful Purging .151

Contemplation: When Stuck, Move. 157

CHAPTER ELEVEN: LIVING SPACE 159

   Attachment .162

      Contemplation: Let Go 165

   Divine Order 166

      Contemplation: Trust 169

CHAPTER TWELVE: WORKING SPACE 171

   Self-Honoring 173

      Contemplation: Inner Power 176

   The Gifts You Bring 177

      Contemplation: Open 178

PART V: YOUR SACRED LIFE 181

CHAPTER THIRTEEN: FORGIVENESS 187

   Responsibility 189

      Contemplation: Powerful Beyond Measure 190

   Healing .191

      Contemplation: Free of the Past 192

CHAPTER FOURTEEN: COMPASSION 195

   Love 198

      Contemplation: Self-Love 199

   Meditation 200

      Contemplation: One with All Life 202

CHAPTER FIFTEEN: YOUR UNLIMITED NATURE 205

   Willpower 208

      Contemplation: Putting Willpower to Work 209

Ask and It Will Be Given 210

Contemplation: *My Power to Create*. 214

CONCLUDING THOUGHTS 217

APPENDIX 221

AFFIRMATIONS 223

PRAYERS 229

Acceptance .230

Attraction .231

Compassion 231

Creativity .232

Emotions .232

Faith 233

Forgiveness 234

Intention .235

Listening .235

Right Livelihood 236

Love 236

Organization 237

Positivity .237

Possibility .238

Practicing the Presence 239

Silence 239

Trust 240

CLOSING PRAYER 241

Acknowledgments 245

PREFACE

The wound is the place where the light enters you.
—RUMI

As you run around with a multitude of personal and professional duties to attend to each and every single day, you are left with very little time to discover new practices and strategies in ways to help you become better organized. Compounding your overly busy life, today's advertising persistently bombards you and challenges your sense of wholeness—think of all the things you "need" to be adequately successful, nourished, well-appointed, clean, sophisticated, masculine or feminine, and the like. You get caught in a web of acquisition that makes it increasingly hard to stay or (for most readers) get organized.

Rather than reaching out, which is what your society has taught you to do, you can learn to reach inside, turn your attention to yourself, and find nourishment in the moment where desires leave you alone. Most of your problems begin in your mind, so let's start there because what you desire is never derived from outside—it all lies within. I approach my life from a spiritual perspective, believing that anything I can imagine can be a possibility in my life. Spiritual problems need spiritual solutions. For example, I say to myself "As I wait to hear the clues from within me, I can open up my mind to the possibility of being organized." You live in such a noisy world that it can be hard to hear that belief, never mind act upon it. You have the power to change your relationship to your things and your time when you operate from a present moment that is steeped in choice and recognize that there are infinite solutions to your organizing woes.

This book, *A Mindful Life: A Spiritual Guide to Making Peace with Your Mind, Time, and Space,* was written to give insight into how to create such a place. By creating a calm space within that allows you to feel rejuvenated and in sync with your deeper self, you can create an easygoing, grounding, and organized environment. Drawing from contemporary spiritual insights, this book will discuss how your thoughts dictate your experience. The constant thinking about organizing in a negative way gives energy to it, and it encourages more chaos in your life. Therefore, let's examine what your thoughts are and see how you can seek a new way of being at peace in your surroundings, where your environment and the way you go about things support you in all that you desire to be.

Staying centered in your personal place of power and feeling connected to your goodness are some of the ways to experience a deeply lived and fulfilling life. Many books have been written about spirituality and how to achieve a better quality of life, but they ignore the importance of your relationship to your inner self to successfully take control of your time and space. On the other hand, books about organizing invariably focus on traditional ideas and methods; they provide acronyms for every organizing solution but don't really address the underlying issue. A lack of organizing knowledge or experience isn't the problem.

A Mindful Life presents a plan that merges the need for structure and coherence with spiritual principles, a system in which the choices that you make are conscious decisions to diminish outer chaos and bring personal power and control over your surroundings. By examining your most basic and fundamental lifestyle choices, *A Mindful Life* describes how you can draw a plan for structuring your inner peace and set up a lifestyle that supports your professional desires. Mindfully created organizing systems for your time, possessions, and space can add value and peace to your life. Once I realized that even I could get organized and I took the time to understand how to lighten my load, a clearer path emerged, and I could see what was mine to do in life. It brought clarity to me, and I could finally see the next steps.

I've been a professional organizer since 1998. A key career goal of mine has been to elevate the conversation about organizing—directing it away from cleaning to clearing, from tricks to deep personal work, from chronic chaos to everlasting peace. How you structure your time and space impacts how you go through life; it affects every area. In my prior books, *Organizing for Your Brain Type* and *Every Child Has a Thinking Style,* I described a method by which the revelation of the readers' natural personality traits can help them to discover and implement an organizing strategy for their time, home, and office. From this perspective, to succeed at organizing and giving shape to chaos, each person needs a method that complements his or her intuitive nature. As discussed in *Organizing for Your Brain Type,* the four types are Maintainer, Harmonizer, Innovator, and Prioritizer. These books aimed to move the organizing conversation beyond cleaning and decluttering with a focus on understanding one's natural abilities, knowing oneself, and learning to work with one's natural traits and desires in order to tackle disorganization. Both books evolved from a deep desire to explore human behavior and to provide readers with guidance in assessing which organizational style works best for them. I knew I was onto something, as no other organizing system had used a personality examination as a framework for the individual's path to organization. I thought they were revolutionary, immensely helpful, and moving my profession toward a more meaningful discussion.

After many years, I still receive weekly e-mails from readers who appreciate the discovery of their own personal organizing style and feel free and liberated to do things their own way. There is no one style in getting organized—everyone is different, and it can be useful to account for those differences in the furtherance of the individual's progress and sustainable success. However, since writing those books, it has become apparent to me that there is yet another, perhaps deeper, dimension that needs to be examined.

I believe that by moving the discussion toward a more spiritual direction, you can obtain sustainable solutions to your organizing concerns. Feeling connected and grounded to what is in your life and being able to connect to the abundance and freedom that are within, can be your saving grace in living an organized and meaningful life. Despite the ephemeral burst of energy you may experience when you earn more money or buy a new sofa, these circumstances don't effectively impact how you truly feel about yourself. When you're honest with yourself, you recognize that the peace and happiness you seek comes from within and that nothing needs to be purchased or consumed. My goal is to help you create an environment that nurtures your vision for your higher self and all that is possible for you, and to spend as much of your time in that internal place of peace and contentment.

Rev. Dr. Michael Beckwith, a New Thought minister in Los Angeles, once said, "We become what we are, not what we want or have." Haven't you, at one time, finally gotten the new thing that you so wanted—a car, a partner, a particular job—only to find that the thing desired didn't change you the way you thought it would? Being attached to a particular thing or circumstance is not liberating. What can be really life changing, however, is having a mindful relationship with what we think about, what we surround ourselves with, and how we relate to our daily activities. One of my mantras is, "I free myself from the need and burden of stuff and am open to the creative vibration of the universe to fill me up."

Remember that at the end of the day, your life is about the quality of the experience you have and how you can bring as much love and kindness as possible to your activities. It's not about your record collection or memorabilia. *A Mindful Life* addresses how you hide your incredible self behind the clutter of stuff or the chaos of time. It will help you understand why you make the choice to cling to stories about not enough of this (time) or not enough of that (space), when in actuality, you have more than enough of both time and space to create a successful and rewarding lifestyle. As Ernest Holmes, founder of the Science of Mind philosophy, once said, "We are bound by nothing except belief." This book is designed to set you free by helping you examine your organizing story with awareness and truth and develop a better relationship with time and space at home and at work.

The search for peace of both mind and one's surroundings is a constant quest for most of us, especially in today's super-busy, goal-driven world. If you find yourself lost in a maze of busy-ness, surrounded by chaos, then the timing is absolutely right for *A Mindful Life*. As you will see in the upcoming pages, by turning within you can develop an understanding of your true potential and of the support the universe is giving you when you just put forth your desire. By having an abiding awareness of what resides at your center, an awareness of the person who is steady, constant, and positive, you will create an environment that reflects that truth.

Creating such a space, one that is supported by the Spirit and encouraged by the soul, requires you to direct your thoughts in a specific and productive way. When you learn to do the *right* things, rather than a lot of things, you will able to take control over your day and thus, your life. Join me in this metaphysical approach to evaluating yourself in relationship to time and space and in the understanding that behind the veil of daily events there is a source of good that intercepts your life: You always exist under the grace of God. Organization begins in the mind, and you can learn how to develop a positive, productive mind and know that you are supported by everything around you when you do. The path only leads upward from here, an opening to learn from and grow into who you think you are and what you can become.

PART I

ON EARTH AS IT IS IN HEAVEN

Heaven on earth is a choice you must make, not a place you must find.
—WAYNE DYER

I find that many people I speak with today feel mentally strung out and physically exhausted, to the point of being depressed, suffering from some kind of addiction and isolation. Experiencing heaven on earth can be a challenge especially when you're constantly late for work, missing appointments, and never able to find what you're looking for when you actually need it. When you're in panic mode and worried about something that shouldn't generate that much stress, you're unlikely to remember the quiet place of rest that is there for you. In this place of peace, there is no concern about "the best use of your time;" you won't feel in constant need to have the latest and best in all areas of your life—the latest iPhone or the newest pair of winter boots will not be of high interest. In this place, you have time to slow down and connect to the presence that lies within. As the American psychologist Abraham Maslow once said, "The sacred is in the ordinary; it is to be found in one's daily life—in one's own backyard."

It is very challenging to make the time to slow down and experience heaven on earth when the "earth" aspect clamors so persistently for your attention. Like everyone, you undoubtedly allow yourself to be overcome by the incessant number of things that tug on your sleeve: perhaps you impulse shop or volunteer when you already have too much to do. I'm sure that you insist that you live up to countless external demands. Do you really need to "be busy" every waking moment? Do you really need a gaggle of people to "like" your photos of your trip to the shore?

I used to repeatedly think "there's never enough time" until I learned how valuable it was to give my words some attention. Truth be told, my former tempo was killing me. I knew that being organized and mindful of how I go through a typical day could help me calm my nerves and make things more enjoyable – but I just didn't have enough time to figure it all out. I find that it is quite easy to allow my day-to-day demands to rob me of the life I imagined, and the more challenged I am by my schedule and deadlines, the less likely I am to have any sense of peace. I must remind myself to hold onto the awareness that doing more doesn't equate to a peaceful life.

You likely try different strategies to feel like your life is working and to give you a greater connection to the life all around you. But these solutions aren't permanent and ultimately, you again feel the void and the powerlessness, robbed of your joy and the wonders of life. So, you vow to try harder, pedal that bike a little more emphatically, and hope that this time you'll break through to the heaven on earth where you're happy. But without taking the time for true reflection and to practice positive, nonjudgmental thinking, you will never lead the happy life that is awaiting you.

Every single day you make choices about what to consume and how to spend your time. I believe each one of them either moves you closer to your dreams, or further from them. Being organized and cultivating a practice of keeping the day-to-day trappings of your life entwined with something that is deep and meaningful is a spiritual process. To gain this kind of mindfulness, I recommend developing an awareness of what is the right activity at the right time. When you do, you begin to enjoy the heaven on earth that your life really offers. Chaos can be conquered with self-awareness and insight into how you go about living. iCal reminders are not enough!

It's ironic that today's conveniences have created a lifestyle that ultimately hampers organizing. Most people are slave to their electronic gadgets. You needn't surrender to the seeming demand that you stay perpetually connected with every news source, every Twitter trend, and every human being that you've ever met. You actually can log off for days at a time—try it! You'll become more aware of your actions, slow down, and develop a great sense of personal empowerment. What you need much more than relentless "stimulation" is the realization that your life is already abundant with numerous blessings and with an awareness of the reality that your current needs, and indeed many of your future needs, are already met. What you need to know is how to create an environment that allows you to be at peace in your mind and in your heart.

It occurred to me that I could help people create such an environment by merging my two complementary passions: spirituality (American metaphysics) and organization/time management. I felt that New Thought philosophy offered solutions to organizational woes that were not well known, and that I could introduce them to a wider audience. I started writing this book many years ago. At that time I lived alone and had ample time to write. I would typically help clients organize their offices and give lectures for the first two weeks of the month and spend the last two weeks of the month writing. But with the emerging demands of raising a family and having many extra commitments tugging at my sleeve, I had to let go of the idea that the book would happen quickly, even though I was sure that the concepts needed to be expressed. I became more cognizant that the little choices I made in my life either gave me more or less freedom to write. These simple choices began to drive my actions.

I realized that by making the right day-to-day decisions, I would have the freedom to do what my heart needed to do—*to write again.* I had to be patient with the process, and to keep my mind on what I truly needed to accomplish. I love the expression, "If I can see it in my mind, I will see it in my hand!" I could see my book completed, but I knew there were a lot of hurdles to jump before it was on the store shelves. I trusted in divine timing and knew that I had a great deal of power to construct a functional, balanced lifestyle. I did, in fact, have the time to write, to do what makes me ultimately happy. Because I've created an environment that is mindfully balanced, I can access the greater insight that brings peace to my life.

I'm convinced that you're here to discover the nature of your essence, to reveal the love that's at the center of your life and the peace that's at the center of your mind. You should aim to do whatever you can to find that place of centeredness, where time stops and you feel connected to something deep within. Organization can be a joy, as it sets the stage for the identification of what's important to you and for your easy access to it. It might sound like hyperbole, but a well-organized, peacefully-paced day really does make the experience of heaven on earth much more likely!

We are all familiar with the quote from Socrates, "The unexamined life is not worth living." He was encouraging each of us to engage in an inner search and to reach a place of self-reflection where we can get to know who we are and be at peace there. My aim is to merge that search with ideas on how to improve your day-to-day choices, using spiritual concepts as a basis for an organized life. In spite of the widely-held belief to the contrary, there *is* enough time. And there is enough stuff—undoubtedly way more stuff than you could ever reasonably use.

You have the potential to move ever deeper into a relationship with your own sacredness. When you get in tune with your own natural rhythm and heart-center, you can gain access to a deeper experience, a life that acknowledges what is, and a knowing that in all your challenges you're not alone. You may not realize it on a conscious level, but you are in a constant state of evolution and self-actualization. Make your mind your ally in developing a pattern of effective organizational choices, and in turn your spirit will be free to pursue its greatest joy.

Your life can be propelled by freedom and characterized by happiness. You're open to discover new avenues for the expression of your joy. When you do, your dreams become a reality. When you want to change something, it's usually because you're dissatisfied with the condition or with the feelings associated with it. What you may not think about is that when you make a change in consciousness, it will affect more than just the thing with which you're dissatisfied. If you want to change something on the outside it all begins on the inside. There is a natural connection to your source, and it is your job to allow it to flow into your life. You don't have to be anything else, and you don't need something outside of yourself to be successful. Just moving toward the light of organizational possibilities will uplift your spirits. The work to do is within, in your consciousness, accepting that you are whole, complete, and perfect just the way you are and allowing your heaven on earth to reveal itself to you.

CHAPTER ONE
THE POWER OF CHOICE

*All doubt and fear must go and in their place must come
faith and confidence for we shall be led by the Spirit into all good.*
—ERNEST HOLMES

A fundamental premise of the New Thought philosophy that underlies my approach to life and organization is that you have a lot of influence in your life - the direction you take and many of your successes occur because of the choices you made. Your notion about organization comes from you, and you reinforce it by how you live it. You are the one that developed your own organizing style, from bare necessity or what you experienced growing up (for example, how the adults in your life were organized). Your experience of disorganization is not an effect of random events, it is the consequence of your actions. You are creating your current life experiences with what you choose to think and how you choose to feel about the past.

By understanding your feelings and choosing to have positive thoughts about conquering your disorganization, you will feel the blessed sacredness that is all around you. The Hindu scripture Bhagavad-Gita states, "The mind acts like energy for those who don't control it." Your mind is yours alone, and you can control it. You can choose to see your life in a positive way, bless what is, and hold a vision of the future that is balanced and nurtured. Even though you're frustrated about your present lack of organization in your life, that is okay. You have a starting place. Turning toward what needs to be healed is how all change begins.

Organizing is a learned skill, not an inherent trait. You have the power to change your life—you choose the organizing experience and then everything around you will shift to honor that choice. That is how powerful you are. You must first fully understand how powerful your thoughts are, and then combine that power with a positive emotion reflecting that which you want and love. It is that simple. Most people think and talk about what they don't like, what is missing, or what the problem is, rather than talking about what they do like, what is present, what is working now.

It is so easy to be negative and critical of ourselves when we want to get organized. According to New Thought writer Neville Goddard, "Do not waste one moment in regret, for to think feelingly of the mistakes of the past is to re-infect yourself." Goddard was wisely reminding readers that dwelling on their previous poor choices does nothing but further the impact of those choices on them today. When we can learn from the poor choices rather than dwell on them, we move in the right direction. So, what if you've felt unable to get organized in the past? It doesn't matter. You're much better off in choosing to think happily about where you are right now. Throughout this book, I'll discuss how powerful it is to simply be positive. I'm not talking about a disingenuous Pollyanna-style smile but rather simply seeing the glass as half full, or seeing an open space. Choose this new way to be in this world, and you will feel the support of the universe.

You are always free to begin anew. Remember that it takes a very dedicated person to look at something that isn't working and see the spiritual truth about it. At its core, getting organized is less about the number of color-coded containers in your attic than it is about how you choose to see your ability to be and stay organized. Tough stuff! Make the choice to see yourself as succeeding when you are getting organized and hold onto that mental picture as best as you can. William James said, "The greatest factor in any undertaking is one's belief about it." Just having that one thought is enough to point you in the right direction.

It's not surprising that the belief in the power of positive thinking arose in America, a place of hope and optimism for what is possible. Raised in the American heartland, Ohio-born Norman Vincent Peale, author of *The Power of Positive Thinking* stated: "Formulate and stamp indelibly on your mind a mental picture of yourself as succeeding. Hold this picture tenaciously. Never permit it to fade. Your mind will seek to develop the picture. Do not build up obstacles in your imagination." Thus, you attain success when you remain confident in your own ability to shape-shift your experience right here and right now. When you choose to be positive, you're using that current of energy to support you and take you to a place beyond your dreams. You may not know how to organize all your stuff, but the right ideas, people, and experiences will appear and help show you the way. Your eyes are now open to choose what you need in your life to help you develop an organized consciousness, knowing deeply that what you think about you bring about.

It can be a big shift in your perspective when you realize that you are the one in control of your experiences. I'm not saying that you "cause" all the things that happen to you. The point here is that you are responsible for how you respond to what occurs in your life, what needs to be healed and which next steps can bring you closer to God. This is your most significant and dramatic power. If you choose to label something as "good" ("Yay, I knew organizing my space would make me calmer and happier") or "bad" ("Dang, it's going to kill me to figure out how to organize my papers in my office"), you then create an experience in alignment with that belief. Your choice about your attitude in getting organized is either going to help you or hinder you—why not see it as putting you on the right path to succeed?

Taking this idea one step further, you could choose to simply accept and be at peace with whatever is, rather than label it at all. For a host of reasons, people often choose to "fight" what is happening around them and to label it as "bad": They respond negatively to things around them, think negative thoughts, and so have negative experiences. They perceive organizing as a nuisance that requires extensive effort. If this describes you, you have a lot of company. Unfortunately, these habits can't help but move your life into directions that don't serve you. When you decide to get organized, you just have to trust that you can do it and find your way. Life is responding to you—nothing is happening to you from an external force. Therefore, focus on things you desire rather than those you fear. Desire an organized life, and it shall be.

You hold many keys to your happiness. If you hang up your responsibility at the entrance to your sanctuary, you'll forever stand at the doorway looking in. You have the power to make the right choices for yourself, and with those choices, you can create a life that is the manifestation of heaven on earth. If you want an organized life, a life that you feel would be soothing and peaceful, then you can have it. The first thing you must do is decide that it is possible, that you will live that life that you so want to be yours.

Perhaps you, too, have arrived at a point where you're no longer willing to make the same mistake again. If so, claim that feeling and tell the universe that you're ready for a new experience. The universe will hear your pleas. With your action on circumstances, something will change; something new will be created. You need to be confident that you'll be successful at being timely and that you have all the skills and ability to create a life that is orderly. Don't focus on the material items that you don't have but rather on the good that you've already manifested. Choose to focus on the good. Decide that you are prosperous now.

To hold a mental image of your new space, what it looks like, how you feel in it and how it makes you function is all you need to start this process. If it is hard to conjure up that image, then you can find pictures in a magazine or a book and place them in a strategic place where you can begin to see what is possible. Don't hesitate to create a vision board; there is a lot of merit in building one. I have mine on my desk, and I look at it at least several times a day. It helps me to "wash my mind" and ignite it with the resolve to stay organized and thrive in that space.

While contemplating spiritual solutions for day-to-day problems, I am always surprised how easy it can be to turn one's thinking (and experience) around. I recently had a session with a client who was having serious organizational issues. I asked him what the opposite of clutter was. He said, "peace and freedom," and then I asked him what that felt like and he said, "I don't know. I really don't feel those feelings often." After we'd spent a good amount of time together considering what an organized life would feel like, he described it as, "a peaceful space, where I feel deeply connected to myself and to all that is in my life." "Wow," I thought. "Organization means self-respect and a good quality of life to him." He never saw the depth of what organizing offered him and now that he desires peace, it will show up in his life and be a demonstration. Now his job is to nurture those feelings, knowing that he is capable of creating that physical reality. He must believe it first. He is now choosing to see himself as someone who's life is organized, peaceful, and living mindfully.

Deciding that you're a failure for being overwhelmed by your disorganization and belittling yourself will never deliver to you the experience that you desire. Many people allow their everyday problems to overwhelm them, and they make no effort to overcome them. I've had clients who have tried for years to "get it together," and there is always something that blocks their good from appearing. Some of my clients had decided, at a subconscious level, that they didn't deserve a life of ease and beauty. And their choice showed up for them in the disarray in their homes and their schedules.

I recently had a conversation with a dear friend who claimed that she was tired of being late to every event she went to, especially her volunteer commitment at her kid's school, which is a rigidly scheduled place. She's permitted obstacles to control her, and her old stories to define her. She sees herself as "the creative one," the one that lives outside the parameters of the establishment. Now her stories have become true, and they have become the dominating factors in her thought patterns. She has decided, "I'm just a late person by nature. I'll never be on time." And with that choice, she's right. She never will. There is no magic to making changes in the way you live. Step one is deciding to see the possibility of manifesting an organized life. The power to choose the best situation is completely up to you.

· · ·

CHOOSING SUCCESS

Your life is not a problem to be solved but a gift to be opened.
—WAYNE MULLER

You might be amazed at how soothing and peaceful it is to refrain from judging yourself and others harshly. Of course, you may not always "hit the target," but that doesn't mean that you need to see yourself as inferior. By focusing on your weaknesses, you set yourself up for failure. When you attempt to get organized in this negative state of mind, you will have an immediate sense of inability and frustration, telling yourself that your efforts are bound to come to naught. Believing in the negative will only beget negative experiences.

Many of us weren't raised to be optimistic. In fact, as young adults, being happy wasn't something we talked much about. Media today seems to be consumed by countless examples of sarcasm, cynicism, and "snarkiness." Being happy, positive, and joyous is often deemed either disingenuous, naïve, or at best, uninteresting. Many people have not been taught how to be kind and nurturing to themselves or to others, and our media-driven culture tends to discourage the development of these qualities.

If you choose to label yourself as bad or inferior, you suffer. Your life suffers, how you contribute to the world suffers, your relationships to others suffer, and on and on. This pattern is something the Buddhists discuss at great length. In their belief system, suffering and stress result from one's incorrect thinking about things, which they call *dukkha*. One form of *organizing dukkha* that many people have is that they're going to be unsuccessful at getting organized. This is a major, core choice that you may repeatedly make, and it will drive your subsequent experience.

Have you ever kept an old item that's broken because you "couldn't bear" to get rid of it? Or kept a gift you didn't use because to dispose of it would somehow be an insult to the giver, or erase him or her from your memory? Take a moment to examine the strange mental gymnastics so many people (maybe you!) go through to rationalize holding on to things that have no purpose, and block your path.

Such behavior doesn't make any sense to an onlooker, but the decision to keep what you have at all costs can often be considered grasping at the familiar to create the illusion of stability and safety. How liberating to be free from this dukkha, this incorrect thinking. The Buddha is reputed to have said, "I have taught one thing and one thing only, *dukkha* and the cessation of *dukkha*." Buddhists believe that the cessation of *dukkha* can be achieved through the power of your mind. When you change your thoughts, you are able to change the course of your life and no longer attract things that cause your suffering.

The concept of dukkha is at the core of New Thought philosophy. The choice is yours to turn your life around, to change your belief that external things and mindless pastimes are going to ease your pain. Every option is a choice for you to make, and you can choose to move to a greater idea of what is possible. When you release the idea that you're inferior to others (and the idea that suffering is the lot you deserve), you move toward a more natural way of being. You're in touch with your true identity—a spiritually empowered realization that results in positive experiences in your life. The cross you bear is that you think you aren't good enough; you don't have the ability to truly alter your experiences, and you fight hard to justify your self-imposed limitations. Have you ever said, or heard someone else say, "I can't help it, that's just the way I am." I would argue that such a statement is rarely true. You *can* help it. You simply need to release the story of your impotence and decide to give yourself the opportunity for a healthy sense of self to arise in your life.

Because you are creating your life experiences with your thoughts, it pays enormous dividends to be fully conscious of where you're directing your attention. The thought-producing machine is always on. You must let go of these beliefs that no longer serve you and awaken to the idea that you're capable of tapping into your ability to carve out a new lifestyle, a different understanding of time and space.

There are no shortcuts in the passage to a deeper understanding of your essential being and the unlimited power you hold to shape your experiences. Be bold, and make that leap in consciousness that being organized is a real, major possibility in your life, a constant presence that you can have. When you decide to reject your sense of inferiority and the suffering you generate, you can embrace the healing wisdom that will serve to create true peace of mind. Holmes once said, "The universe holds nothing against us—there has never been an occurrence for which we have to suffer." Choose courage, choose to believe in yourself, and know that you're ready and open to receive the answers and solutions to your organizing problems. Know that you deserve this experience and that you will gain enormous insights from it. Believe in your success, and you will achieve it.

Remember, this book is about shifting consciousness, shifting your awareness to heal what needs to be healed in your organizing world. Give yourself five to ten minutes to answer the questions that follow. The exercise will conclude with an affirmation that allows the above ideas to be put into action. This will be at the end of every section. Take the time to do the exercises—don't rush. You should repeat the affirmation until you feel it entering your heart and changing how you feel. Let your emotions be the guide. Starting with your thoughts and analyzing your thought patterns by using the techniques outlined here, you can modify the circumstances in which you now live, open up to different stories of possibility, and cure the thoughts that keep you feeling like you can never get organized.

* * *

Contemplation: Listen to Your Soul

I quiet my mind and open my heart.
I breathe in and out several times.
All is quiet and all is well.

- What is your mind telling you right now?
- What do you most want to act upon?
- Who should you seek out to help you?
- Where do you go next?

Take the time to listen to your inner guide. When you are inspired by something, there is a reason why. Perhaps you need to organize your closet to allow space for a future partner to arrive, or to eliminate some commitments from your calendar, so you can take the trip that you always wanted to take. Let your creativity lead you to a place where you are inspired and overjoyed with what lies ahead. "Stop, look, and listen" to what is guiding you in getting organized and to the challenges you now face. Be honest, don't judge, and become quiet to listen to your next organizing steps.

Affirm: *I'm in gratitude that I choose to have thoughts of joy and am* *successful when I begin to organize my life. I believe in possibility. I believe that the Spirit will guide me to balance my life. I believe that the right organizing solutions will present themselves. I believe in myself and turn toward the light, healing my mind and liberating my space.*

. . .

A POSITIVE WAY OF LIFE

I am open to positive change.
I free myself from fear and concerns about
my ability to get organized.
I am willing to forgive myself and
move from the old to the new.
I am grateful that I have the insight, and
I embrace my new organized life.

Positive thoughts create positive results. Yet, the minds of many people generate a stream of negative mental chatter that influences their daily experiences. Peale claims, "These so-called 'little negatives' clutter up the average person's internal (and often external) conversation, and the total effect of these attitudes is to condition the mind negatively. The best way to eliminate them is to deliberately say a positive word about everything." You should try to do this consistently. Try it even when it doesn't feel true, as you'll find that over time, you're increasingly comfortable seeing and articulating the good in everything and everyone you encounter.

For myself, to dissolve my negative thoughts in any situation, I personally say, "I accept that right now is a new moment in which anything is possible, and being organized is my new way of being." I then make the affirmation more pertinent to what I'm specifically undergoing, such as, "I am well organized. I relax and let this idea fill my entire being with new and vibrant energy. I affirm that all negative attitudes are now dissolved, and I go free to live this day constructively with wonderful experiences." What I'm doing is shifting my attention in a new direction (dropping the idea that "Oh, this is bad") and choosing to implement my own potential and abilities.

Nothing from the past can block the divine flow of good and the boundless possibilities that are available to you. It's up to you to simply have faith in your abilities and let your instincts guide you, as your newfound self-confidence will lead to success and joy creating a lifestyle that uplifts your spirit. Organizing can be a challenging undertaking filled with heavy physical action and self-criticism. Changing your mental attitude and adopting a strong belief in yourself, you can release your inner powers to their maximum potential and manifest what you have imagined.

In other words, you must keep your concentration clearly on each needed step as you progress confidently toward your goal. Find people that support this vision you have for yourself. Staying positive is staying on task; you never want to diminish the idea of what is possible. Remember that anything you can imagine is yours to be or do or have. You are choosing your thoughts, and in turn you are choosing your emotions. As the American philosopher Henry David Thoreau suggested, "The secret of achievement is to hold a picture of a successful outcome in mind."

The doorway to greater possibilities and positive change is always open. The Spirit within always says "yes" to your desires and demands and provides the avenues for you to attain your organizational goals. The barriers you experience are invisible ones that you've allowed to live inside yourself. You may not even be conscious that they are there, but they have a tremendous impact on your life.

And until you are willing to release and move through those barriers, recognizing your unity with all of the qualities of the divine, you won't be able to truly manifest your greatest future.

To move through the barriers you've created to your fuller expression, you should look honestly at the times when you didn't achieve your goal. You should consider what qualities you needed to draw upon in order to have been successful, and begin seeing yourself as possessing them. Once you've envisioned yourself as fully capable, and claimed the truth of your divine nature, you can decide the right course of action to take. But know that you don't develop magical abilities through your positive thinking. My former minister would say, "You must treat (pray) and move your feet!" So, if you desire to get organized, you first must believe that you can do it and then actually start doing something – however little it may be.

That last idea is critical—you must also do what needs to be done to make your dreams a reality. Try the following: a) conjure up a mental picture of yourself succeeding at getting organized, b) immediately voice a positive thought if any negative thought emerges; i.e. "flip it around," and c) refrain from building stories that justify your past actions. The Dalai Lama once said, "In order to carry a positive action, we must develop a positive vision." Be aware of the thoughts and people that are entering your space. Always ask yourself, "Does this uplift me or make me feel depleted?" Tune into the frequency of what is possible rather than what can't be done. Turning towards happiness and joy are your barometers that you are moving in the right direction.

* * *

Contemplation: Surround Yourself with Positivity

I quiet my mind and open my heart.
I breathe in and out several times.
All is quiet and all is well.

Cast negative things away from your environment. You'll want to have as much positive energy around you as possible as you move in the direction of seeing and affirming the positive in your world. Start with bringing your attention to the good that is in your life—even if it is something small. I recommend doing everything you can to surround yourself with positive people (limit time with that friend who complains about everything!), reading material (inspirational books are great to encourage you and assure you that the universe is a loving place), and the like. All of these things send out an energetic vibration. You are constantly making choices; choose to make positive ones.

Affirm: *I am positive and excited to create new organizing systems and to bring a greater awareness to this concept in my life. I stay connected to the truth of all that I am and all that I need and desire. I am experiencing an organized life right now. I'm in control and inspired by my new surroundings. I'm grateful for this experience.*

CHAPTER TWO
LAW OF ATTRACTION

One's mind should swing from inspiration to action,
from contemplation to accomplishment, from prayer to performance.
This would be a well-balanced existence.
—ERNEST HOLMES

American metaphysics, the foundation for contemporary New Thought beliefs, was first made popular in the nineteenth century by visionaries such as Mary Baker Eddy, who founded the Christian Science movement, and Charles and Myrtle Fillmore, who founded the Unity Church, along with many, many others. They all shared the belief that you can heal yourself with the power of your mind; and by training your mind to see things positively, you attract the right experience into your life. They all believed that a good attitude helps you not only attract the right experience but also makes you a better person. According to Charles Fillmore, "God is not a being of love and wisdom, but a force of attraction."

A key premise of modern metaphysics is that there is a force of divine goodness in the world, and it is ready to support you when you ask it to do so. From Ralph Waldo Emerson to Emma Curtis Hopkins, metaphysicians contended that you could change your life for the better by living with the expectation that your life will continually get better; and you could "think" your way to health, happiness, and fortune. This practice requires complete, unwavering belief; and the ability to be positive, use the law of attraction, and expect the good to arrive at any time is the real work.

As we've discussed previously, a positive frame of mind is needed to accomplish anything that appears difficult, and that includes getting organized and living a life that is organized and at peace. How do you do this? An example would be to first allow a deeply felt intention for ease and peace in your space and calendar to manifest within your consciousness, knowing that as you do so, you are already beginning to establish the desired outcome. By creating the mental mold for the experience to occur and walking in faith until it does, you are using your mind to change the internal rather than the external. That is how change begins.

You are meant to have an incredible life; you were not put on this earth to struggle with your stuff. You deserve a life that is comfortable, beautiful, organized, and peaceful. You deserve a home and work environment in which you know where everything is, that is attractive and inviting, that is welcoming to all who enter. This is the vision that you must hold and employ when you want to get organized. This is how you begin to use the law of attraction. My mantra is: "Be it and you will then see it!" Be firmly convinced that it is possible and you will create situations that will only support that vision.

Your belief in the possibility is what the universe (or the divine goodness I referred to earlier) hears and responds to. You must remain positive, sticking with your beliefs as best as you can. Start the ball rolling with these thoughts: "My life is organized, and time is my friend. I attract and bring forth things in my life that are well organized." You can inspire change to happen by using this brief affirmation. It is particularly appropriate when you're feeling pulled away from being organized.

As I said in the first chapter, if you want to change how you live and how you experience the world, you must begin with the thoughts you have about yourself and your expectations. If your thoughts are directed with great expectation on what has yet to arrive, they become a powerful force of attraction. You must expect the things you want and not concentrate on or put energy toward things you don't want. Since every negative thought, feeling, or emotion is blocking your good from coming to you and the shortcut to anything you want in your life is to *be* and *feel* happy now, do it! According to Charles Fillmore, the universe is "right with you all the time and responds to your faith in it and your demands on it."

It is vitally important to remember that you have the power to choose what kind of life you want—you can have an organized and peaceful life or a cluttered and chaotic life. Because there is nothing outside of yourself that is limiting your future, you are responsible for much of how your life takes shape. Your thoughts are very powerful; you're bound to make a point of deliberately determining what kind or quality of thoughts you want to have. It is a big shift for most people to acknowledge that they alone are at the controls. But by doing so, you begin to really see that you have a lot of say about how your life turns out. Thank goodness you have this ability, this freedom to choose what vibration to send forth. I've always said organizing is 10% mechanics and 90% self-esteem. Use the power of attraction, and if you truly believe that you deserve to have a balanced life, you will have one.

The law of attraction, or what I also like to call vibrational choice, is a very basic concept of New Thought philosophy. According to the metaphysical law of attraction, you see that like attracts like—negative thinking brings about negative results, and positive thinking brings about positive results. Ernest Holmes once said, "We must trust the invisible, for it is the sole cause of that which is visible." One way to understand it is to envision your thoughts as "magnets" or "seeds." Whatever kind of thought you are having, you are then attracting like thoughts to you. It is another way of saying that what you focus on grows. For example, if you shift your thoughts toward happy and successful organizing endeavors, your experience will match what you are thinking. What you choose to focus on expands, you are free to create new.

American philosopher Wayne Dyer said, "The central notion of manifesting is the understanding that you have within yourself the ability to attract the objects of your desire." It is an amazingly powerful law, similar to gravity—while you are on earth, here in this moment, you are subject to it. The force that makes your ideas about organizing a reality is brought about through the law of attraction. (You are always using it; it is always turned on.) Initially this may seem intimidating that there is a power that responds to us. However, when you realize that you hold many of the keys to your own happiness, it is liberating as only you can change the direction of your life.

Indeed, the law of attraction is the law of love. What you send out you receive back. Loving yourself is the greatest way to improve yourself. You can heal whatever organizing problems come your way. To best employ the law of attraction, you must figure out what will help you generate the feelings of now having what you want and how to stay in that mind-set while you wait for your desires to come to fruition. Learn to do whatever you have to do to generate the feelings of having what you desire now, and you will bring into your existence everything that you require. You work with one infinite power, one source of all creation that is able to shower you with all that you need.

A person cannot think thoughts such as "I can open all this mail tomorrow," "It doesn't matter where I put it," "Oh, I always forget to set my alarm," and experience an organized life. According to Holmes, "We cannot live a choiceless life. Every day, every moment, every second, there is choice." You want to begin having thoughts of confidence and determination in order to create the experience of a newly organized life.

The Spirit of intelligence and unlimited bounty that wishes to express itself through you surrounds you all the time. The divine urge to connect with something larger is always present. You are at the source of the river, but you must let down your own buckets if you wish them to be filled with the pure waters of organization and peace. An immutable law of cause and effect also surrounds you, and you experience only what you really believe and act upon. Remember the choice to think positively is always yours. You must cast out of your consciousness every doubt and every sense of un-certainty that exists around what you want to change, such as your relationship with organization. You must believe that you are en-tering into an atmosphere of wholeness; having complete faith in the ultimate reality of structure and peace that is arising in your life. The organizing possibility is stirring within.

You shape your own destiny by the management of your thoughts and feelings. You must meet your good halfway, by becoming that which you desire to manifest. You must be it to have it. If your predominant thoughts are on the success of organization, what that feels like and means to you and to those in your life, and you know that only good organization and nothing else exists in your mind, you will be victorious. Your predominant thoughts of organizing are what bring organization to you. This is the law of attraction at work.

On the other hand, most people are thinking about what they do not want. When you focus on the things that you don't want: "I'm invariably late," or "I never pack the right things on a vacation," the law of attraction takes you at your word and manifests those thoughts in reality. That is why people experience the same problems or misfortunes over and over again. The law of attraction is not biased as to "wants" or "don't wants." By emitting defeatist energy, you get struggles and difficulties in what lies ahead. Find the glimmer of light in getting organized, feeling and sensing how much easier your life will be, and it will appear in your life. It is frequently described as impersonal, meaning that it isn't concerned about whether it delivers a good thing or a bad thing; it's just a natural consequence.

If you desire greater order and greater peace of mind, you can say, "I am so grateful for my order and my peace of mind." Once again, the law of attraction is at work—as you focus on order and peace, they will come your way. By giving your attention to being better organized, you have activated a thought vibration within yourself that will initiate the process of becoming organized. That is how you start.

• • •

VIBRATIONAL CHOICE

The energy of the mind is the essence of life.
—ARISTOTLE

Contemporary New Thought philosophers see that our lives are continually evolving from choice to choice and that everything in this universe is working on a vibration. Since everything (yes, everything: your fingers, your dog's instincts, clouds, money, dust, music, electrons, cars) is a form of energy, just holding a different notion of something in your mind shifts and changes all things around you. Change the vibrational tone, and your situation will change to match it. You are the one that chooses the frequency. There are countless energies available to you at any given moment, and you can always choose a higher vibration if you so desire. I might argue that the greatest power you possess is your power of choice. The vibration that you're sending out is bringing everything into alignment.

And so, the energy that you're emitting, the hopefulness and happiness, sets the organizational process in motion. What if you can't find that hope within? What if nothing but feelings of defeat arise when you contemplate an organizing project? Well, then your job is to simply fake it until you make it, to give out the highest vibrancy possible. By doing so, you pull in the divine support you need to be successful. You don't have to know everything or have luck on your side—the quality of your experience is driven by your thoughts and the energy you're sending out.

I tend to see our bodies like radio receivers, sending and receiving vibrations masked in the form of ideas. As you think, you are vibrating, and as you vibrate, you attract. The thoughts and emotions you have about something are all vibrational in nature. By turning your attention to a higher frequency, to the direction of light, love, and goodness, you will find that divine grace and love will enter all your actions. Like attracts like, so the longer you hold a positive thought, the greater the number of positive thoughts you have—and hence the greater the number of positive experiences sent to you by the universe. Use your power of choice to select positive thoughts and feelings when you're getting organized. You will attract what you send forth.

All that is needed from you in this process is to: a) close your eyes; b) breathe in and out; c) listen to your thoughts and acknowledge the feelings emerging from them. I'm a visual person, so I "see" my feelings in colors. I know when I feel "red" that I have to breathe a bit and calm myself down. By doing so, I shift into feeling "purple," a color that I connect with joy and harmony. In a state of "purple," I'm aligned with God and able to rise above my fears. Yes, you can deliberately generate a feeling that is lighter and more positive, and this is just one of the many ways in which to accomplish that goal. Simply by shifting your attention, you're able to change the vibration and, hence, what you're outputting into the world.

❊ ❊ ❊

Contemplation: You Are Receiving What You Are Giving

I quiet my mind and open my heart.
I breathe in and out several times.
All is quiet and all is well.

The laws of the universe return to you what you send out, and they don't take sides over your positive or negative emotions. Remember that the universe is always ready to act in accordance with your commands. You are always being responded to; it is always creating, and it never stops. See your thoughts as boomerangs, immediately coming back into your space and creating the experience that reflects them. Like everyone, you are operating on a frequency.

Affirm: *I'm consciously aware that what I give out comes back to me. Therefore, I hold the highest and best for others and myself, knowing that I* *can be well organized and that I will be successful in creating and maintaining organization. The universe is a place of order and balance. Since I am part of this universe, I know that my surroundings reflect that order and that balance now. My life is in perfect order.*

. . .

MENTALIZATION

The premise upon which all mental work is based is perfect God, perfect man [woman], perfect being.
—ERNEST HOLMES

The ideas that you have about your organizational abilities must come from a place of desire and possibility that lies somewhere within you. The life that flows through you takes the form you give it, and the form comes from the thoughts you have about it. Eventually, you come to the conclusion that everything outside you is a reflection of your own thinking. It can be a daunting realization that what you mentally seek, seeks you.

So, when you take that wisdom and apply it to your organizing situation, you must change not what is being projected (on the outside) but rather change the projector itself (on the inside). Therefore, the wishes you have to eliminate chaos and to be appropriately scheduled will begin to take form because you desire them to; you *will* them to be. I see it as using your mind as a cookie cutter; cutting from the entire divine good and shaping it into the form in which you want it to materialize in your reality.

"Mentalization" refers to the idea that whatever you desire has to be somewhere already existing in you, or you wouldn't have thought about it. You cannot bring forth something in your life that you're unable or unwilling to mentally hold as a possibility. Do you want to be better organized? Then, feel that harmony and peace within when you are cutting out your experience. A life that is free from chaos, unnecessary interruptions, and constant stress over the mundane is possible for you as long as you're mentally holding the vision of that possibility inside of yourself.

How do you go about this if you are experiencing anything but an organized, peaceful existence? First, let's articulate your desire or vision for your new life. Perhaps you'd like to get all your paperwork in order or organize all your electronic files for work. Affirm that your desire to organize is already happening and shifting things in your life, now. Since your desire is fueled by energy and the sheer joy of an organized experience, see the task completed. See it as sustainable and easy to maintain. Frame that picture in your mind, and all the right experiences to live within that framework will emerge. Mentally prepare your mind for the best, most powerful, and magnificent organization to be part of your life now.

Whatever your desire is, it is your job to embody it until you see it manifest in your life. If you put a concerted focus on what you want in the forefront of your mind, it has to take form in the physical realm. Be specific in your vision. You more powerfully change your organizing situation for the better by doing this than you do by buying new organizing toys. Know exactly what you want. Imagine peace at work in lieu of chaos. Imagine flowing gracefully from one event to the next in lieu of a frantic, inflexible schedule. Surrender to your vision, and trust that things are moving in the right direction. Ernest Holmes agrees with this approach, saying, "All doubt and fear must go, and in their place must come faith and confidence, for we shall be lead by the Spirit into all good."

Assistance in creating the right mental framework may come

by using affirmations when feeling overwhelmed. I like to focus on a concept or a specific phrase when I want to change my life in a particular direction. As I mentioned earlier, ease and grace guide my organizing efforts. (Most people think about things that they don't want, and sure enough, they keep getting the experiences that confirm the truth of those thoughts.) You are always thinking thoughts—either ones that support your higher self or ones that diminish what is possible.

The universe responds to your thoughts, so think the highest and best in regard to how your life will be organized. What are you gaining from being in control of your surroundings? What are the blessings going to be for those around you when you are calm yet vibrant in your life? When you're in the flow of life, it doesn't rule you if something is urgent or should have already been completed. You can get things accomplished and remain at ease, all the while attracting what is right for you at that very moment.

In every minute, you're either expressing a larger concept of life, of what is possible, or you're remaining stuck in poverty and limitations. Whatever you desire, even though it may seem far-fetched, like "getting the house organized by the Fourth of July" is a real possibility. Your belief in yourself, that you can do it and be in control of your surroundings, is where you need to start. In time, that organized house will appear in your life. If your vision inspires faith and action, you're on the way to manifesting your wish as a reality. An organized life *is* possible. You have to desire it, and think it, to have it. Act accordingly and see your power carve out your organizing path.

* * *

Contemplation: Visualization

I quiet my mind and open my heart.
I breathe in and out several times.
All is quiet and all is well.

Allow God's presence to comfort you. When you find that you are focused on a situation that causes you panic and worry, immediately stop and focus your attention on the feeling of God, turning your mind away from the problem and centering your thoughts on organization, beauty, and peace. See a structured, attractive environment, at home and/or at work, surrounding you. Internalize that vision and send it back into the universe. See it, believe it, and return the thought. With this, you put the law of attraction to work. Declare that all organizing solutions and the right items to make them manifest are in your life now. If at first you struggle with this vision, keep at it. Stick to it until you feel it, and you will be transformed. What does your newly organized office or in-box or filing system look like? Feel the passion and joy you get from it.

Affirm: *Today, I am deeply filled with confidence and a sense of peace. I am actively aware of the presence of the Spirit within me, guiding me in expressing myself in a greater, more organized way. I'm centered on the possibility of creating and sustaining an organized life. I know that I'm drawing the right ideas, tools, and inspiration to achieve my desire.*

CHAPTER THREE
FORCE OF GOOD

When you realize that nothing is lacking,
the whole world belongs to you.
—LAO-TZU

The final metaphysical element for your organizing project to be successful is the knowledge that there is a force of good in the world. Your job is to know this intimately and use it when building a new understanding of organizing and structure in your life. There is no God in the sky passing judgment on you and no person preventing you from accomplishing what you set out to do. Stories of how you were raised in chaos, or that you've never been on time, are just stories; they are not who you have to be. It is up to you to release yourself from the power that these types of stories have over you and to refuse them a place in your mind.

You have the power to turn around any situation. You're born with the genes to succeed, to grow, to become intimate with your good. What frequently holds people back is the belief that a force outside of themselves isn't their friend; it judges them and doesn't support them. This couldn't be further from the truth. What lies outside of you is a force of good; a force that is there to assist and comfort you in times of distress or concern. You immediately let in light when you turn toward this force that wants you to express your highest and best good. In so doing, you turn away from the past, from your prior, negative view of things and beliefs you were once taught that do not uplift you and support you. You create the momentum to move toward the divine good, filling the void that occurs when you leave the negativity of the past behind—you create a space from which healthy new thoughts can emerge.

Believe that the best is yet to come, and you are healing a sense of separation from your sacredness. You are given every opportunity to heal yourself and your life. To claim this perspective and allow it to color your life is a big deal—it was the game changer for me! This isn't a mental exercise, but rather the sense of a calm, loving presence that supports you in all you decide to do. (If you want to name the loving force of good "God," that's perfectly fine. I intertwine both words, God and good.)

The force of good is always with you; you are never alone. It is always there; just listen to your heart's intentions, and allow it to help deliver that which you want. It only supports and loves you in all that you want to have in your life. If you are conscious of this divine force of good and you use it, you're aligned with a very powerful source from which to improve your life. This force drives the creative process; how ideas take shape and begin to appear in your reality. There is no one in judgment of your thoughts. As German author Eckhart Tolle puts it, "Your primary purpose is now to enable consciousness to flow into what you do."

For the most part, our present-day culture dismisses the notion that the source of all creation is loving and wishes for us to succeed. No matter which challenging situation you may find yourself in, it is your job to imagine and feel that the best outcome will happen for you. The process is the same for whatever you want to change. Anything that does not support this idea or support your achievement of what you want—be it a friend or a choice—must be released. Remember that the universe operates on vibration, and putting the best and most loving thoughts into it will create a desirable outcome, one in which you are in control of your environment and time becomes your friend.

• • •

FAITH

It does not make things easy; it makes them possible.
—LUKE 1:37

Having faith, as understood in a metaphysical sense, means two things: a) knowing that the source around you is loving; and b) knowing that it wants you to succeed. These ideas aren't part of most people's upbringing today, and so a big inner shift must occur inside you before those two things really become part of your reality. When I use my imagination to envision an organized life, I know that I must walk in faith until I see that organization occur. If you can imagine it, feel it, and believe it, you will receive it. Being positive and trusting that you can do it may be all you need to get going and to find excellent solutions in your home or office. When you trust your own ability to create what is possible and have faith that the force of good will respond to your vision, you are in a powerful position to enter a new world that resides within, a world that is infinite, free, and loving.

With deep faith that all is moving in the right direction comes a sense of ease; things appear out of nowhere, and joy and happiness enter into your life. "All you can possibly need or desire is already yours. Call your desire into being by imagining and feeling your wish fulfilled," says Neville Goddard. My faith in divine goodness calms my mind and gives me hope. When you discover and trust the force of good, inner wisdom feels free to come forth into your consciousness, and thoughts that exude the fullness of life enter your head and shift your surroundings. To have faith is to believe unfailingly that the best is yet to come. Then you can simply get on with your life by giving yourself as much love and as many good feelings as you can. You can turn away from the thing you don't love and give it no attention. It then loses its power over you.

You can rely on the above metaphysical principles to simplify your life. Remember to hold fast to them and that you can't be single-minded about feeling good if you're a) chasing your tail over little things that don't ultimately matter or b) worrying about future events that you fear will come to pass. By eliminating your focus on nuisances (stop sweating the small stuff) and all the "what ifs" that haunt you, you create the space for everything you want to pour into your life.

The universe is responding to you. As one of my ministers once said, "As we turn to God, God turns to us." You can learn to become powerful by taking your own word seriously and being open to the changes that will follow. Don't be consumed by your demanding schedule; take the time to feed a deep connection to the truth that all is unfolding for your betterment. Stop. Breathe. Feel connected to yourself. It's worth it because what you give your attention to becomes your truth. When you allow your connection, you thrive.

Remember that the universe doesn't respond to just your words but also to the vibration that you are transmitting.

* * *

Contemplation: Quiet Your Mind

I quiet my mind and open my heart.
I breathe in and out several times.
All is quiet and all is well.

Take the time to be alone either early in the morning, before you go to bed, or better yet, both. Relax your muscles. Mentally seek out good experiences you've recently had that bring a smile to your face. Breathe slowly, creating a space in the mind that allows for other positive experiences to emerge, and reflect upon them bringing you joy and peace. Then bring a desire into your mind. Feel it, explore it, know that it is possible, that it is going to happen and be a part of your life. Have faith that goodness surrounds you and awaits you, and that you are moving in the right direction. Allow yourself to be swept away by good energy, motivation, and joy.

Affirm: *I am one with the Spirit of God. I have faith in the power of my thoughts and an organized life that I can have. I believe I am successful in my new endeavors. Although the precise organizing systems I will employ may not be clear to me now, I still believe that I'm being guided, and I'm receiving answers and solutions to my organizing situation. Through the power of the Spirit within me, I achieve my dreams. I prevail and overcome any negative organizational issues.*

• • •

Transformation

My realization and acceptance of my current organizing situation
propels the thoughts and actions that will transform
my consciousness now and in the future.

Everyone is a part of a natural cycle of transformation. You do your part; you pray, meditate, and study spiritual texts. Behind the scenes, the universe is doing its part, acting on your behalf through the creative power of your thinking. Then *voilà*! You change your old habits into efficient new ones and create a happier, more fulfilling life. You find simplicity and order within yourself and in your home, and they nurture your soul. You realize how important physical peace is to your spiritual growth and start to value and prioritize it. When you desire something, that desire just becomes part of your journey in living a reflective, conscious life. You have the gift of peace of mind because now that you know where things are, your space is tidy and organized. The changes you're experiencing are supported by your faith in the endless divine good that responds to the picture you hold in your mind.

When you are living according to your truth, the divine principle of life, all is in harmony. Even though there is a shift and things appear differently, you are still constantly transforming, creating another new experience to be nurtured in (and to learn from!). This creative gene exists in everyone; our lives are meant to be creative. I even have dear friends who have founded their careers on this principle. Their business, "Life Artistry," helps those who want to express themselves playfully map out a better life plan. What could be more fulfilling than treating your life like it's a work of art?

Embracing the new, not being fearful of change, is going to liberate you on this organizing journey. Don't worry! The first steps feel scary, but when you open up and turn to your true desire with an open heart, the right plan will emerge, and you will only see good things as a result. Just turning in the direction you need to go and taking that first step is critical. This is how transformation happens. It may not feel natural at first to praise and bless the good in whatever circumstances or conditions arise in your life (especially when they seem adverse on their face), but to do so is certain to bring about a shift in your experience. When you move from negative thinking into positive expectancy, you attract the good that is always inherent and available to you, and you transform how you experience what happens to you. Sometimes wonderful solutions and life experiences come out of what seems at first to be a misfortune.

I lived for decades believing that things just happened to me; that I was always at someone else's, or some other force's, mercy. This was a very disempowering belief system, and it is one that people who are poorly organized often hold. Organization is about the mindfulness you bring to time and space and how you structure your day. When you're moving through life with belongings that just bury you, you leave no room for anything new to land in your life. If you clog up the movement of divine energy with all your stuff, you block new possibilities from entering. It really is just common sense, but if you could see the actual energy all around your things, it is likely it would encourage you to act differently.

If you truly trust that the divine good is waiting to help you transform your life and that the best is yet to come, you will then capture the organizing zeitgeist once and for all and see it as the blessing that it is. By taking the viewpoint that organizing is of benefit to you, rather than oppressive, you can appreciate it and discover your organizing style. If your space supports your soul, then all is well. If not, then transformation is in order. Remember that the only thing permanent is impermanence and even with organizing systems in place, over time, even better usage of your space is likely to emerge. Let your desires light the way, and know that the coming change is a good thing.

Transformation can be uncomfortable. It requires focus, energy, insight, and a determination to see it through. If there is light within you that knows how much better you will feel once you're organized, great! That means that you're open to let the light into your life. I've heard many times that when one door closes another opens, and I heartily agree with that maxim. Your life is about to change—close the door on resistance and fear and allow optimism and confidence in your ability to straighten out your home or office to take hold.

How fortunate you are to be open to a new start; what a gift you've been given. You've moved in the right direction by surrounding yourself in gratitude and forgiveness as you release your old beliefs and open yourself to the nourishment of grace. You can trust that something better will replenish you as you let go with courage. My motto is always, "The best is yet to come." Believe that and know that any change to your life is for your greatest good. By embracing and respecting the change that is about to happen, you can ease into your new experience with the calm knowledge that the highest and best is materializing. Welcome this change in, and trust what you are hearing inside will create the best possible organizing system for you. You can tap into this powerful source of creative energy when you're willing to cultivate a sense of order in how you conduct your daily affairs. Experience this energy in thoughts of your own well-being, and wait for the transformation. You are a sacred human being with unlimited power to change your life.

* * *

Contemplation: Beginning Something New

I quiet my mind and open my heart.
I breathe in and out several times.
All is quiet and all is well.

You have the energy and desire to master a certain aspect of your space or your time. Beginning slowly but consistently, see and trust the magic of embracing a new venture. With passion and purpose, let go of all thoughts of limitation; release worry and the need to control each step on the path. Know that you are guided and led into the next best thing that is right for you. You now trust your own abilities, know that your inner voice will guide you in the right direction, and have faith that the universe will show up with all possibilities made available. Be positive about organizing and know that the change that will happen can only make your life better.

Affirm: *I trust the next step that is laid down before me, as I know it is guiding me into a great next possibility. I welcome ideas, solutions, and support in my organized, conscious lifestyle. Today, I put into practice what I know will support my overall health and well-being, and I call in order and experience it in my life.*

• • •

You're ready now to venture into the discussion of gaining control over your mind. As you do so, remember the three powerful metaphysical principles that we've explored thus far. First, you have the power of choice, which allows you to focus on being positive in claiming an organized life and to turn away from your old stories. Second, the law of attraction is reinforcing your thoughts. The thoughts you have about organizing (and about everything else!) are coming right back at you in reality, affirming their truth. Your job is to believe in your organized life's truth until you experience it. Third, the universe is a force of good, and it acts on your behalf.

To support you in your organizing efforts, the universe requires that you be open to changing your behavior and believing in your own success. With these principles as the foundation, let's now turn to mastering your mind, your time, and your space. By gaining an understanding of your true relationship with the universe, you will be able to address your earthly organizational woes with heaven-based solutions.

PART II

YOUR MIND

I am not what happens to me, I am what I choose to become.
—CARL JUNG

People's problems begin in their heads. They blame situations, experiences, and others for making them unhappy and unsuccessful at organizing. It is always someone else's fault that something has gone awry. It is always someone doing something to them that spin them in the wrong direction, and that is why they live amongst chaos. That seems true if you don't analyze the situation deeply but in fact, it isn't true. If you truly look at your stress and anxiety and at how crazy your life feels, you'll see that you yourself, not a situation or an experience or another person, are creating those problems.

When you see that your unmet desires and soulful unrest arise from within, you're on your way to becoming free. But because you are in constant motion, it's hard for you to understand what's going on inside yourself, for you to see how your very own consciousness is either moving you forward or causing you to suffer. Like most people, you're undoubtedly addicted to busyness; you take very little time to seriously slow down and to make conscious choices about how you want to live. You believe that "things happen to you" rather than believing that your thoughts and expectations are sending out signals as to what should occur in your life. This includes your success at getting organized.

When you're feeling low or vulnerable, it's unlikely that you ask yourself, "How can I respond differently to these circumstances?" Instead, you leap at old patterns and thoughts and simply reinforce what doesn't serve your highest and best self. It is probably that you have a history of deeming the source of your organizing issues to be outside of yourself, and then buying 100 percent into that story so that you can't even get off first base. But when you turn toward that which is challenging, you find you have the strength to rise up and use your divine intelligence to find solutions. In this section, I will look at how you can make changes by understanding the power your thoughts have over manifesting and creating an organized life. I'll also discuss how understanding the power of your intuition can free you from fear and lead you to accept your organized and fulfilled life.

In our world today, it is hard to find the balance between mindfulness and mobility. As Deepak Chopra said, "The pursuit of human's existence on earth is to master the art of living in the two dimensions—conscious doing." If you allow yourself to examine the busyness of your brain, I bet you'd find that your mind believes that it has to keep in constant motion—with compulsive thinking and judging. And most of what you think is not only untrue, pointless, and repetitive, it's also downright damaging!

If you're lost in your thoughts, and you let them pull you into an unhappy state, you've let them take the lead. You've given up control, and you've set the stage to experience stress. Here you go. The stress shows up, and you try to overcome it by some extreme action. Perhaps you overwork, overeat, drink too much, or engage in excessive shopping. Perhaps you devote unending hours to playing a game on your computer, or you just sleep more than you need to. No matter what the behavior, it doesn't further your well-being. You can examine what is really at the center of the disharmony in your life, and decide to change it.

When you are overwhelmed and feel despair, sadness, or anger, you can be pretty sure that a specific thought is causing these feelings. You may want to believe, for example, that you're angry because your spouse once again left the dishes undone. "He (or she) makes me so mad!" you think. And so, your spouse is responsible for your feelings, right? No. Your spouse didn't do anything to make you mad. Dishes were not washed. You chose to respond by getting angry. You could have chosen to just, without emotion, do the dishes or asked your spouse to please do so or by ignoring them altogether. Your thought that went something like, "Arghh, why do I always have to clean up?" is what made you feel angry.

Similarly, if you feel guilty about something, such as the lack of peace in your surroundings, you can assume that the guilt arose from your anger or judgment about your current situation. Since everything you do begins in your mind, anything you want to change comes about by the thoughts you have about it. Therefore, your initial desire to get organized comes from within. The solutions along with inspiration will make themselves known.

As I suggested earlier, however, it's hard to see clearly how you generate your own suffering because like all of us, you're way too busy meeting the demands of your job and family. In this section, I will examine the way in which an unsettled mind takes shape in your outer world as chaos, disorganization, and stress. If you want to change anything in your life, you have to start within and take full responsibility for what you're manifesting. Joel Goldsmith states, "As you close your eyes in prayer, God knows that it is for the purpose of being an instrument through which his grace has reached your consciousness." Goldsmith was encouraging readers to go within and be still in the quiet center of their minds, where they can really hear their inner wisdom.

And so, by far the best way to resolve your organizational woes is by studying your thoughts and understanding that they are at the center of your surroundings. Being at peace with what is around you begins with being at peace in your thoughts. Surrounded by a positive, loving force, allow yourself to be open to seeing things differently and doing things differently. Your thinking is all that you need to change—it is the only thing that you can control. You need to get your mind in order before you get your stuff in order. In my many years of helping people get organized, I never saw their circumstances as the organizing problem. Something within themselves attracted this organizing situation.

So, I ask you to turn within to that universal presence that speaks to you, where you hear the voice of your inner wisdom, opening you to a place of deeper understanding of your feelings and the beliefs behind them. Ernest Holmes wisely said, "Divine ideas stand back of all human thought, seeking admittance through the doorway of the mind." Listen, and be guided to a conscious realization of the truth that an unlimited supply of good is available to you and that when you clear your old mental chaos, you're expanded and renewed. There is lots of space in your mind for what is truly important to you and what kind of experiences you want to have. When you know why you do the things you do, it will become much easier to decide what to keep and what to let go of.

Chapter Four
Understanding Consciousness

The supply for every need or desire begins in consciousness.
—Ernest Holmes

I 've heard many teachers say that the joy of being alive is the joy of being conscious! What do we mean by the word "consciousness"? When I talk about consciousness, I mean an awareness of our mental connection to our physical actions—our mental perception of our existence. You can experience yourself at a superficial level, stumble along from one emotion to the next or one attempt to seek comfort to the next, but that is not living at a high level of consciousness.

Being truly conscious is having all your mental facilities open, moving you in a direction in which you always feel connected to your center. By being deliberate and intentional in how you lead your life, you will see who you really are, what your true needs may be, and how you can feel happy, organized, and complete. Neville

51

Goddard said, "When you know that consciousness is the one and only reality, you are free from the belief that there are causes outside of your own mind that can affect your life."

What does consciousness have to do with organizing? Well, everything begins in the mind—the idea you send out into the universe becomes realized in your actual physical surroundings. When there is mental clutter—such as beliefs of failure and lack of supply—the creative process brings forth an experience that is in accordance with that belief. This is probably one of the most important chapters in this book, as you're asked to look deep within to see how your beliefs and your expectations manifest and take a physical presence in your life.

There is a programmer in your life, and that programmer is you. There is no one person, entity, or situation that is controlling you. Your external reflects your internal and to see what isn't working all around you requires you to begin within. Your beliefs and feelings are the source of the framework you create and the contents of the picture you fill it with. Your beliefs come from somewhere inside of you, telling you who you are, what you need, and what you are capable of. If you're like most people, the majority of the stories you tell yourself aren't good, aren't helpful, and aren't very kind.

The Vietnamese Buddhist teacher Thich Nhat Hanh compares the typical human mind to a wild horse, going in whatever direction strikes its fancy. I love this image because it always reminds me to stay on the path! Like wild horses, people race from one thing to the next and they don't process what they're experiencing. The American author Byron Katie once said, "Our problems are not the cause of our suffering, but rather the thinking about our problems is what causes us great pain."

As you grow and evolve in consciousness, you learn to be more authentic, and you allow yourself to be governed by your heart and not your past. Stories of how you will never be organized and that you will "always be that way" take up valuable space in your mind, justifying not taking the next step. If your mind tends to go in that direction, you'll want to take a hard look at those thoughts. Do you repeatedly engage in that type of thinking? Your beliefs give direction and purpose to your creative energy and that is what shapes your experiences. These experiences, in turn, further "the truth" of your beliefs. By telling yourself that you'll "never be able to sort through all those papers," and then finding that the task is so daunting that you stop after five minutes, you confirm the "truth" that you'll never be able to sort through all those papers. Your belief becomes reality.

When you complain and express a desire for things to be different from what they are, you strengthen your ego, the part of yourself that is constantly craving, constantly wanting something other than what you're actually experiencing. You affirm "the truth" of your grievance. For example, if you tell your friends or yourself, "I can't help it, when I'm on the computer time just slips away," you're also telling the universe that you can't control how you spend your time; time is something that's bigger than you are. The universe responds in kind, offering you a never-ending array of opportunities to mismanage your time. You are then unproductive, unfulfilled, and unhappy. All this arises from your mind, not from the circumstances in which you find yourself.

Everything is consciousness manifesting, and if you don't like what you see, you need to shift something inside to ensure that this outer appearance doesn't stay around. The minute you get attached to your thoughts, and invested in them, they turn into beliefs; they travel out and take shape. It is your attachment to your beliefs and stories that cause you to suffer. If you can mentally step outside your thoughts and observe them, you'll be shocked to see their longevity and the "logic" behind the stories that go, "It can't be done. It's not possible for me to be successful at organizing."

The reason that you can't do something, such as being organized or work out in the morning before you leave for work, is that for years you've told yourself that the task is too big or too hard or you're busy and don't have time. You've decided that there isn't anything you can do about it.

Life continues on this way in an ongoing reflection of your evolving (or non-evolving) consciousness. The darkness is not real. Only light is real, and it is always available and present for you. A conscious perception of wholeness and perfection dispels the darkness and lifts you into the light of truth. The first step is to think about the negative story you've been telling yourself and then write down an opposite statement about your organized life: Close your eyes and sit with this question for a moment or two before you read on. What language best speaks to your story? Perhaps you want to write: "I know everything I need to know to organize my papers," or "I have all the time I need to clean out the garage." If you can think about what you want as often as possible and picture, for example, an organized bedroom in your consciousness, your imagination, which began as a mere mental image, is changed into solid reality. An organized life is possible for you. You can do it. Believe that truth with me.

• • •

BELIEFS

Everything is possible to those who believe.
—Mark 9:23

This mental clutter of old ideas, habits, and ways of existing in the world continually affect your choices and behaviors. As you move into the future, you're lead by old beliefs about who you are and what kind of life you can expect. Regardless of their origin, these beliefs shape everything you experience. They shape your life in ways that you perpetually create in your mind. We are made by our beliefs. As we believe, so we are. So, if you want to change something on the outside, like a cluttered environment, you have to first examine why that chaos exists and why the "need" for chaos has been created in your mind.

Your beliefs typically distort reality. All concepts, judgments, and opinions about how you're to proceed in getting organized come from what your beliefs are. When you're just reacting to events and others, rather than actively directing what you're thinking, you abandon an uplifted version of yourself. You're on autopilot, sticking to old beliefs that keep you in the past. Beneath the judgments that you've impressed into your brain, you can often find other thoughts that you've held onto for years, and that you use as the "truth" about your life. Your version of who you are has been masterminded by your thoughts. And so, change is possible with just one thought. Your healing is that close to you.

Building confidence in creating a sacred life is about building a new belief system. First, believe that you will be successful at getting organized. No matter what people have told you or how your family lived, you are free to have the lifestyle of your dreams where you feel safe, organized, and happy. Second, believe that the right person, the right ideas, and the right organizational solutions are around the corner, coming in your direction. (Even if you have a hard time digesting this one, you must stay the course until you either believe it or see it appear in your life.) Lastly, believe that the peace you seek in your space is now coming from a peace within; the peace in your mind and heart is making the outer appearance match the internal.

Purging the mind attic is not for the faint of heart. Just like you, wherever I go, I collect and affirm beliefs about myself. They sneak around disguised as "simple realities," but they harbor anger, frustration, hopelessness, and more pain than you or I could ever imagine. As you study the origin of your thoughts and the actions that you take, your awesome power of choice comes into play. You're free to keep or discard thoughts, both those that are disheartening and disempowering and those that are making you feel at peace and happy.

I have three quick go-to tips that always readjust my beliefs from something negative into something full, abundant, and peaceful. Using these may seem disingenuous at first, but I suggest trying one or more of them. They're great when you experience turbulent emotions and find it hard to see the good at a time of struggle. The first thing I do is immediately assign a letter grade to my performance in regard to anything I find scary to do. If I think I'm a B+, I up it to an A-. If I think I am a B-, I assign myself a B. Just a little notion like this puts me in the right direction and makes me believe more strongly in myself. Second, I always have a picture in my head of myself succeeding at the task. Even if it seems as if it would never happen in a million years, I see it coming to fruition. Third and last, when I start to have a self-defeating thought or a worry about the future, I immediately stop and say a positive affirmation to myself. I might say something like "I'm on task to conquering my incoming mail," or "An abundance of good surrounds me and supports me in dealing with my paper now and at all times."

A happy life exists within you; you need simply to go in and draw it out. Ralph Waldo Emerson once said, "A person is what they think about all day long." Since you make up your beliefs, usually relying on something that is false about a situation, you can easily change what is currently happening by deciding to have a different belief about it. Check in regularly with the beliefs you have about yourself. Are they supporting you in getting organized, or are they serving as speed bumps to your success?

The only thing that keeps you down is how you perceive yourself. Many times over the years I've heard highly negative stories from people that justify the reasons for their disorganization. "I never learned how to keep things in order," they'll tell me, or "A cluttered office is just in my bones." Does this sound like a story that runs through your head? I find that, unfailingly, such stories are masks for different challenges or difficulties that people don't want to face, and that their clutter serves to somehow assuage some fear or loneliness that they are trying to escape. But when they change their belief, deciding that something is positive and most surely possible, they can begin an activity that might seem otherwise out of their reach.

* * *

Contemplation: Believe in Yourself

I quiet my mind and open my heart.
I breathe in and out several times.
All is quiet and all is well.

Let no thought of limitation enter your mind. Turn over your belief system from lack, or negativity, to what is possible now. I think of a coin which on one side sits a negative belief and on the other side sits a positive belief. "Flip it!" Visualize the coin flipping over to the positive side. When a negative thought arises, such as, "I don't know how to get organized," simply flip it and say to yourself, "I have the ability to find organizational solutions that greatly improve my life. I am changing my belief system." This is a powerful tool to move your thoughts in the right direction that you can take with you wherever you go.

Even if these thoughts strike you as disingenuous, that you cannot believe them, just say to yourself "So what?" Go ahead and tell yourself that you have the ability to find solutions. Act "as if," and do it anyway. Insist upon your own strength, and you can then make that strength your reality. You cannot allow yourself to be deterred, and if need be, follow the old adage "fake it till you make it." This is the real work that needs to begin to change anything. I'll be the first to admit that it is daunting to get on this horse of possibility. But staying on is not that tough—once you're in the saddle, you will soon have some tangible evidence that new possibilities actually do exist!

Affirm: *My thoughts are full of unlimited expectancy and possibility. I believe that there are good organizing solutions that will enter my life when I need them. The right people will be a part of my organizing efforts. I know I am capable of being successful and organized in my life. I believe in myself and that all things are possible.*

• • •

FEELINGS

Thoughts are the shadows of our feelings.
—FRIEDRICH NIETZSCHE

The fuel to the flame of your life comes from your feelings. My former minister often said, "If you want to know what you're thinking, become aware of your feelings. They never lie." So, if you want to know what you're thinking, ask yourself how you're feeling. The universe will respond to the nature of that inner feeling to create something that reveals it in reality; therefore, you want to feel good.

Find something that makes you feel whole and happy; find a positive thing in your life. When it comes to organizing, rethink your initial reaction to getting organized. Sometimes the initial thought will trigger a negative emotion, like resentment, anger, or fear. Don't be afraid to look that feeling straight in the eye—you're experiencing it whether or not you want to accept that to be the truth. So, you've really got nothing to lose by just allowing yourself to acknowledge that it's there. If the feeling is fear, for example, invite it to reveal the belief that is driving it. By changing the core beliefs that drive painful emotions, we can explore the roots of our actions (or inactions!).

Disorganization and despair about getting and staying organized don't come out of thin air; they come from a belief about yourself that you have now swaddled with feelings. That belief isn't who you are. You have the ability to change things. In time you will see yourself as victorious, and it will only get easier in the future. There is always the possibility of a healing that is just around the corner. Believe in the reality of your desires, and the feelings will change too.

Our thoughts don't act alone in making things happen; feelings energize our thoughts into action and put them into form. What makes you ultimately decide to get organized, to take action, is both the thought that you deserve a better life and the feelings that give your desires urgency. Something right now, within you, desires a shift in regard to how you live your life. You desire freedom and peace in your living space and in your mind. I think the deep desire people have to find this peace energizes their thoughts, and in turn their positive thoughts more forcefully attract the support of the universe in achieving their goals.

You have probably experienced at least some sort of organizational success, and even small manifestations of success count. Think about a past moment in which you got organized, and bring it into the present sphere of uncertainty. Remind yourself of that success and the happiness you got from it. Keep it close by in your imagination and use it when needed. Keep the visualization fresh, as clear as possible, and relive it every day for a moment or two. Cement it in your mind, and let the feeling of successful organization reign supreme and become alive. Revisit these sensations over and over again in order to help keep alive the spirit of your organizing potential and the order that is taking over all areas of your life. Feel the truth of this new reality.

By feeling as if you have already accomplished your goal, you generate the positive perspective with which to do so. Eventually, the more you let your powerful self lead the way with what is possible, your natural inclination will follow with feelings (and a reality!) of success and accomplishment. Set the power into action that will bring you the opportunities, tools, or people necessary to accomplish your goals and finally be successful at getting organized. You needn't live on autopilot, being reactive and living in fear.

Remember to keep asking yourself how you are feeling. Emotions give you a great deal of insight into what you're thinking. A new thought generates a new feeling; the universe matches the tone of that feeling, and what will flow into your life matches the feeling that you're holding. You can release yourself from being a victim from life by always turning toward what is possible. Remind yourself over and over again what is possible, and by doing so, you will generate new feelings and push that belief forward. This sounds very easy in theory but sometimes challenging to do practically. Start off small, noticing a feeling that arises. Explore where it comes from, and say a prayer that is supportive of your higher self. In time, this consciousness will just be within you ready to become what appears in your life. Be joyful that you have faith, knowing that the best is yet to come. Connecting to your heart and listening to what stirs it is the deepest way to bring forth true and everlasting change. To know what you're thinking, ask yourself how you are feeling.

. . .

Contemplation: Feel the Feeling

I quiet my mind and open my heart.
I breathe in and out several times.
All is quiet and all is well.

What is the feeling behind your desire to get organized? What does it feel like when you accomplish your organizing goals? Fill up your conscious and subconscious minds and every cell in your body with the feelings that are affirming your newly organized life. Feel the sense of peace when all that you need is close by, when you know how to locate your spare keys, your plaid shirt, and when all your mail has been opened, read, filed, or discarded. Now feel yourself free, unencumbered, and organized.

Affirm: *I stand brave in my determination to get organized; knowing that being at peace with my space will create greater peace in my heart and mind. I feel this to be my truth and as I become more keenly connected to my feelings, I am better aligned with what appears to be the highest and best in my life.*

CHAPTER FIVE
THOUGHTS ARE THINGS

It is necessary that we release all thoughts—
as well as things—that clutter up our lives.
—ERNEST HOLMES

If you could spend just a short time turning inward every day to focus on what you want, rather than what you don't want, you would experience a very different kind of life. Earlier, I discussed how the thoughts you have about your life either propel you toward joy and happiness or confirm your inner suspicions that you're poorly equipped to manage the things that happen to you. Thus, it is the power of your thoughts, rather than the things that happen to you, that has the greatest influence on creating your life. Knowing how to access your thoughts and direct them to the positive and possible is a lesson that can be learned.

Whether you realize it or not, you are thinking pretty much every waking moment. Traditional wisdom holds that people have over sixty thousand thoughts a day, and you'll want to devote a number of good thoughts, especially to something that you are dealing with, like organizing, to be successful. Your thoughts become true for you through the law of cause and effect. Cause is the thought or belief that you send forth into the universe. The thought is acted upon immediately; the effect is the resulting experience that mirrors the thought you planted. What you send out comes back to you and manifests in your life. The good news is that once you change the thought you send forth (cause), the result (effect) will reflect the change.

More often than not, a person's current thoughts and feelings pass without any kind of awareness or direction on their part. These workings of the mind result in the "wild horse" behavior I mentioned earlier. When you want to start living life in a new direction, it takes vision, focus, and work. Send forth the thought that you are an organized person. You will see only positive effects from your efforts, and you will create the environment that you desire.

By seeking out the place between the thoughts, where the sacred speaks, and spending time in the pauses, you can shift your mind from being a reactor to a free flowing, positive seeker manifesting an organized life. I urge you to take the time to step back and look at your mind, with its directionless, compulsive, and mostly harmful thoughts. When you bother to separate your thoughts from yourself and examine them, you can move them in the direction where you know you will experience organization and peace with all that is around you. When you pause and reflect, you allow the sacred to speak to you; your consciousness expands, and you're able to use your thoughts *for* yourself. There is no reason that you can't direct your mind to a positive experience, such as an organized room, and generate the thoughts that let the universe know that you're ready to achieve your goals.

Yes, you are the boss of you, so start giving your mind the right orders to follow. Let's look now at how to positively use creativity and the law of attraction to make sure that what you're giving your attention to takes form in your life in positive, organized, and peaceful ways.

. . .

CREATIVITY

The student should take time everyday
to see his life as he wishes it to be,
to make a mental picture of his ideal.
—ERNEST HOLMES

I always feel that when a new idea of what is possible appears in my mind, it must come from somewhere other than just my imagination. I have to believe that it comes from some power that wishes to cocreate it with me and bring it to fruition. The world contains a creative power that is always in motion. This power dwells within everyone, and it is always creating everything that arises in the physical world. It is always reacting to our thoughts. Albert Einstein said, "Imagination is everything. It is the preview of life's coming attractions." If you can imagine an organized life and feel what that is like, it will take form. Einstein thought that imagination was more important than knowledge. Therefore, align your thoughts with the truth of your creative mind.

Using your creativity to unlock a beautiful and organized life path is your gift back to God. Far too often, people think that this path is restricted to "real" artists, but as Julia Cameron points out in *The Artist's Way*, everyone has the ability to use his creativity and join with his divine source to create something from nothing. When you discover and express your creativity, your artistic connection to your divine source will lead you to design and create your life in a certain way. You will start to see how important it is to be open and to plant the right thought (cause) so as to see the desired result (the effect).

Be aware that the center of your creativity isn't in your brain but rather in your soul, that aspect of you that is most intimately connected with the Spirit. That is where inspiration and desire for connection are held, and where your true or higher self abides, emerging to experience the mystical and divine. Something within you wants to be better organized and seeks order in your space and in your life, and the creativity of the universe is working through you toward the creation of a calmer environment. Don't forget that your higher self has planted the seed, and the change you seek is seeking you.

Your pure essence comes forth through your creativity, and to draw that essence into reality, we must become centered. By calming the mind and centering, we develop a feeling of insight, where we can listen to the path that our better self would like to take us on. Our creative voice can be loud and clear and cut through the air with direction, purpose, and passion, releasing our deepest inner wisdom of organizing solutions.

In most cultures, creativity and spirituality are commonly manifested through music, song, and dance, and these are ways to express the soul's desires and even the joy of being. But creativity and spirituality need not be confined to traditional methods of expression; they show up in every aspect of your life. According to the American philosopher Eric Hoffer, "Creativity is the ability to introduce order into the randomness of nature."

The connection between your thoughts and God's thoughts help your creativity to flourish. Your job is to use your creativity, your ability to tap into and manifest the good of your divine source, to bring you to where you want to go next. When you're dreaming, you're creating something from nothing and letting your higher self lead the way. While it may be a new experience for you and feel uncomfortable at first, you must resolve to support yourself in your new vision, always staying the course and seeking answers from within.

Before I get underway in creating a new thought pattern, I always start with a positive gesture to my current life, blessing everything that has been part of my life up until that time—all the situations I've been in and all the different people that I've met. Each of these things has given me a fuller appreciation of all that life entails. For example, rather than focus on the negative and your unorganized environment, picture what could be.

So, how do you get from your thoughts on what is possible to manifestations in your life? The actual creative process (i.e. creating something from nothing) consists of three steps. First, *claim* what you desire. Let the universe know what you want, color in the picture of how you see your organized life. Second, *act as if*. Feel that what you desire is already yours, that you have it. Think about what is possible rather than what you don't have. Third, *experience* it, as it is now in your life, you are now living what you once only dreamed of.

Relax into the endlessly creative nature of the universe and allow it to inspire new visions and new strategies for your organized life. You can trust and let go, not judging your answers. When I open up to my creativity, I am awestruck by some of the amazing ideas and solutions that come into my head. My personal goal is to spend more time quietly devising my next action steps and answering my creativity's call within a realm of hope and aspiration. (Reexamine the questions on page 18.)

You can draw from the creativity of the universe at any time, and the more you do it, the more productive it will be. The creative power you're accessing is always reacting to you as you draw from it. It is always at work in your body and in your affairs. Consequently, you may confidently live in a state of joyous and enthusiastic expectancy. This is the principle upon which faith or the answer to prayer is based. Go ahead and bless everything you do and everyone you meet, knowing that the limitations of the past need not be carried into the future.

* * *

Contemplation: Be Open

I quiet my mind and open my heart.
I breathe in and out several times.
All is quiet and all is well.

Empty your mind of anything that doesn't support your highest and best-organized life from coming into form. Be open to the infinite creative force of good that envelops you and expresses through you. Open your mind, your heart, and your thoughts to hear and listen to what is transforming all around you. Know and feel your organized life to be part of your life now, and sense things slowing down, the installation of order and peace between all things and all events.

Affirm: *My creativity guides me. I'm still and calm, and can see the direction that my heart wants to take. I listen to my inner guide and accept what is without labeling it good or bad. I'm delighted by this fresh start. I pause before the blank canvas of my life until I feel guided and moved to create a more organized life. I behold and am delighted by the fresh start the Spirit inspires in me.*

• • •

MANIFESTATION

Everything is Spirit in essence, though hidden in manifestation.
If you had the perception, you would see God in everything.
—PARAMAHANSA YOGANANDA

When you are feeling good, you are putting yourself in the frequency of what you really want. Walter Evans, one of the early New Thought writers, once said, "Mental certitude and visualization, backed by faith, is the engine of creation." In other words, positive thought, supported by unwavering belief that the thought is reflected in reality, is the foundation for the manifestation process. How life appears before you is a result of all the hard work you've done to create it. You have, in one way or another, shaped your life by finding the courage to ask for what you wanted, then believing that it could be possible, and finally, experiencing it in your physical reality. Since you can talk yourself into negative or positive results, you might as well take the time to carve out the positive life that you want to have. The only organizing reality that really matters is the one that you create for yourself. Your thoughts can manifest outcomes, and you can and will have that organized life that you want.

Metaphysics teaches something called the law of mental equivalents. This law states that you cannot recognize or experience something in the outer world unless you have an equivalent image of it in your mind. Therefore, you plant potatoes and potatoes you get. This growth process, like anything you plant, requires time and effort—good soil, water, and weeding. So today I affirm, I plant thoughts in the rich soil of my garden. I water my thoughts with faith, trusting in the law of mental equivalents for them to grow.

To bring about an organized space, you need to consistently water the idea of order, trusting the law that order is the truth of that space. In discussing the practice of manifesting one's positive thoughts, Mitch Horowitz, author of *One Simple Idea,* said, "I clung to the hope that one's internal attitude and perspective mattered—that holding the mental ideal of a better reality could help make it so. I emerged from the period believing that a set of interior guideposts and principles had contributed to the solution. If my thoughts didn't change reality, they helped to navigate it."

As you navigate your thought process in relationship to how you're going to get organized and how that could take shape in your life, you might ask yourself, "What is the first judgment I make when I contemplate getting organized?" Where are your thoughts directing you? Typically, the first thoughts people have when starting something new are worry and fear. Unfortunately, worry and fear have become the natural approach to change for most of us, and they destroy the chance of a great takeoff (as I discuss in detail in the next chapter).

In order to manifest something in the outer world, you need to have an equivalent image of it in your mind. Accordingly, you want to center your thoughts on what you want most in life. To bring about better circumstances for yourself, you need to enlarge your concept of whatever you wish to see improve in your life—it has to come from within you to attract it into your physical reality. Prentice Mulford, co-founder of the New Thought movement, once stated, "Your prevailing mood or frame of mind has more to do than anything else with your success or failure. The mind is a magnet. It has the power first of attracting thought, and next of sending that thought out again."

Knowing that you possess the keys to your own organizational freedom will further your confidence. Maya Angelou said, "I did then what I knew how to do. Now that I know better, I do better." Now is the time for you to turn things around. If you see your thoughts as being magnetic and pulling things toward them that match their frequency, then you can understand how your thoughts create your life. How do we then move our thinking into patterns that will manifest our desires?

First, begin by telling yourself that you're not limited by the events or experiences of your past. Stop adding commentary to what didn't happen and situations that got you into trouble. Stay connected to the divine truth of your boundless ability, to the truth of light and love and all that is possible.

Second, form a picture in your mind of what the positive organizing circumstances are. Hold that picture in your mind. Stay with it throughout the day; feel it flooding your conscious mind, your subconscious mind, and every cell in your body with the feelings of living your dream, your organized life.

Third, when you're frustrated and not seeing your life quickly and miraculously getting organized, keep your mind on the Spirit. Remember that every circumstance offers an opportunity to turn toward the light of your own being, leading into your inner wisdom for guidance. When doubt and insecurity arise, banish them from your mind by praying for what is possible.

What you're thinking now about organizing is either positive or negative. It is so easy to say, "Just think good thoughts," but since you have such a tremendous number of thoughts each day, this advice can be overwhelming. Like with any habit, you create it one moment at a time. Rather than get carried away by the seeming endlessness of this new habit, just practice it now. Only you can make it enter and be a part of your life. When your mind is cluttered with frustration, lists of things to do, and ideas that disturb you, stop what you are doing and come back to that bigger picture of who you are and how you see yourself being in the world. Let go of doubt, embrace what is possible, and stay on that course until you have it in your life. God is always there; you are never alone. Nothing is too good to be true; nothing is too much to ask of the universe's guiding force of good. It is your life and your dream to live in a perfectly organized fashion.

* * *

Contemplation: Self-Belief

I quiet my mind and open my heart.
I breathe in and out several times.
All is quiet and all is well.

By cultivating a calm mind, and finding that space between thoughts where I can shift and expand and exist with greater awareness, I reinforce my belief that the best is yet to come. As I plant good thoughts and tend to my garden with perfect conditions, my thoughts grow rich in my soil. I always water my thoughts with positive reinforcement, with more thoughts based in faith, knowing that the organized life that I imagine comes into my reality now. I see things flowing around me easily, in perfect order, harmony, and peace. I don't waste money by buying things I already have. I can now find all that I need and am never without. I hold onto this thought. My life is organized, I feel in control, and I feel happy.

Affirm: *I lack for nothing. I am directing my inner mind to know a greater truth of what is possible in my life now. I recognize that I am one with God, the infinite life of the Spirit, so I let go of limiting thoughts about how*

I'm going to get organized. I now realize that I am free at every moment, and I renew what is possible in my life by renewing my thinking about it. I create an organized life, an organized space where I feel peace and calm, allowing my highest and best to come forth. My thoughts are powerful. I use them in creating an organized life.

CHAPTER SIX
LEAN INTO INTUITION

Our part is to be ready and willing to be guided into truth and liberty.
—ERNEST HOLMES

I have found that much of my untrained thinking results in unfocused busyness, collecting things, and having very little energy left over to deal with all of it. When your energy is in perpetual motion and your thoughts are unchecked, you end up getting into trouble by making unproductive decisions and having to spend more energy dealing with their consequences. It takes a lot of energy to get out from under your stuff to make better sense of it; so, let your thoughts carry you, but let them emerge from your intuition, your higher self.

The wild horse of the mind is a constant way of life in the modern world. As an organizing consultant, I've been in countless environments that seemed so cluttered and full of things; they had been set up in a way that didn't support the basic needs of the users.

I noticed that many basic organizing systems seemed to work against the natural inclination of my clients. I knew they either didn't listen to themselves or had someone help them who created a system that may have worked in a general sense but was not specifically tailored to the user. There appeared to be a disconnect, a lack of flow from following and listening to one's intuition to produce a result that was in alignment with the user of the space.

I wrote in the prior chapter about relying on your creativity for a source of ideas about how to be better organized, and here I'm suggesting that you also turn to your intuition. Just to be clear, the former is a force within the universe that you draw upon and express; the latter is a force within you that is innately yours, alone. Both are inspired by the wisdom you hold within. Your intuition is your personal inner guide to what best serves you. You can lean into your intuition to find the directions for what needs to be organized first.

Therefore, when you feel it is time to release some items that don't serve you, trust what you're feeling and sensing to steer you in the right direction. If you can genuinely learn to trust your intuition, you will begin to experience greater joy and freedom in your life, and this will in turn support your new way of thinking. You'll feel full with the divine creative force coming forth into form and will feel less compelled to spend time engaged in diversionary pursuits that don't ultimately serve you.

Those inner conversations that you have, those debates about what to do and which course to take, may be best resolved by simply asking your intuition, "What is the best choice that will keep me on task?" Then go in that direction one step at a time. When you start demonstrating a life with minimal hiccups, you will see that the flow you are in is happening because you are connected to your deepest sense of self that comes through as your intuition. Before long, your intuition will become your most trusted companion, one that you will value and celebrate as it surfaces within your mind.

When something seems like it was just "meant to happen," like reading about an organizing system that you hadn't thought of, or even finding a great new yoga teacher with a studio only a mile away, take note. Bring about an awareness as to all the good that is happening in your life because you are listening to your higher self and going with your gut feelings to experience a deeper and more enriching life. Before I step into the unknown and call forth what I desire, I start on a positive note, reminding myself of all the areas that I have broken through and in which I've been a success. Then I can ask myself, "What is the Spirit calling me to do now? Am I willing to listen to my intuition? Am I willing to act on what I'm hearing, follow my heart, and do the work that is required?"

As long as your intuition is genuinely coming from your inner wisdom (don't confuse it with old fears and resistance just because they're lurking in the back of your mind!), you're undoubtedly making a smart choice. The purpose of life on earth is to realize who you are and to act and live in accordance with that. Traditionally this had been called enlightenment, self-realization, salvation, or being born again. Evolving to this state of bliss is not something that comes quickly, but the journey is more gratifying than any of the diversionary actions most people devote their lives to. Working toward your own self-realization, your connection to your God center, will give you what you need to be successful at life and really conquer your disorganization.

The path to an enlightened state of awareness frees the mind and awakens intuition and deepens its presence. The stillness of the mind is infinitely attractive to the human soul, and when the thinking mind becomes allied with intuition, the sense of peace and joy exists as your physical surroundings are aligned with a deeper purpose. Be still to hear the guidance regarding how to proceed. Be grateful for the insights you have and for the good that is yet to appear. As you listen to your intuition and follow your heart, change is already happening in your life.

• • •

RESISTANCE

The cave you fear to enter holds the treasure you seek.
—JOSEPH CAMPBELL

You resist taking the first step and trying something new because you're afraid that it won't work out and you will not be successful. You tell yourself over and over stories that justify your inability to succeed. How could things turn out differently? The Indian philosopher Jindu Krishnamurti once said, "Fear is the destructive energy in people." If you allow it to, it can hold you back forever. You resist moving forward; your current situation may not be comfortable, but it's *more* comfortable than delving into the unknown. Your resistance is a choice you make, although undoubtedly a subconscious one. You choose the "safe" route of not changing, the "safe" attitude of scarcity instead of abundance.

The resistance you feel toward organizing yourself stems from old fears that don't speak any truth about you. Your higher self, your intuition, tells you that moving in the direction of an organized and peaceful life is most definitely possible. Just having this insight and wanting it can shake things up and break through your resistance. Holmes once said, "There is no power in the universe but ourselves that can free us." Let your fear become a great teacher, open it up and see what is there.

Why is it that you can hear loud and clear what your higher self is saying, but you resist acting upon it? How can you gather the strength it takes to plow through something, when your wise inner guide tells you that it is the best path for you? Like many people, you find a reason to put off cleaning out the attic; organizing can be such a daunting task. Life keeps moving on, and it is hard to stop and work in the past, with old belongings and papers, much of which should be discarded. You can easily become sedentary, especially when you've grown older, and the physical, mental, and emotional work required to make a difference in your space is tough to find. I know for a fact that it only gets worse if not dealt with—many of my friends are at the age at which they're cleaning out their parents' homes, and the unlayering of the possessions is a long and tedious process. Let's face it, that old desk is not going to be declared a priceless heirloom on *Antiques Roadshow.*

If this doesn't inspire you to let go of your resistance, try thinking about something that you tried for the first time and succeeded at it. Cover your resistance with that memory and let invincibility and possibility open the way for an organized life. When an old concern arises, flip it with a positive frame of mind, and pray. Spend time listening to the wisdom of your intuition, and the rest that follows will be straightforward and doable. Remember that despite the resistance that has become your habit, you are always free in every moment to see things differently, to interpret things in a way that encourages you to be present and willing to be strong.

You can break the resistance habit; it reflects unrealistic ego-based fears. The ego, which drives most of one's actions, is the instinctual part of your mind, taking you back to the caveman period when real dangers, hungry tigers or death from exposure were the driving forces of one's life. Today, the ego is intact and is just as fear-driven, always looking out for the next challenge. When you want to get organized, your ego says, "No way, you can't do that, stay safe in the place you have." How many times have you turned your back on a new adventure because your ego said you can't and you shouldn't? How many times have you resisted making the changes that will free you from the chaos of your life? Befriend your resistance; don't run from it. You will begin to see that it will lose its power over you, and you can get organized once and for all.

Procrastination is not birthed from laziness or lack of resolve. Rather it tends to be a deeper psychological situation involving anxiety, fear of either failure or success, or the product of simple, basic overload. It's no surprise that you resist getting organized! No big deal—jump-start a shift in your thinking by writing about your success at dashing your resistance, write down solutions, get them out of your head and onto paper. Spend the time to figure out how to proceed. Don't surrender again to inactivity; press upon the universe to deliver what you want, and stay steadfast in your dedication to realizing that the job is done!

Growing through your fears is one of the real challenges in life, but when you break through something that has been holding you back, nothing could feel finer. There are a lot of answers waiting to be discovered and seeing what your resistance has to teach you about organizing is how you move through it. Meet it head on, shake it up, and allow your intuition to take the lead. See how things transform in your experience.

It takes strength to stay fully present and to see God as your source in a very challenging situation. But the wish for freedom from disorder can overcome whatever resistance holds you back from living a fulfilling, joyful life. Instead, you must surrender to your spiritual essence, believing in the goodness of God and trusting a universe that is on your side. Fear doesn't serve your highest and best. Be open to the possibility that is before you and know that you have all you need—the creativity, the intuition, and the faith in all possibilities—to ensure you get the job done in a way that you can sustain.

. . .

Contemplation: Trust

I quiet my mind and open my heart.
I breathe in and out several times.
All is quiet and all is well.

Your inner guide never misleads you. Move into a greater sense of trust and belief in what is possible. All the vision and ideas that enter your mind help you move forward and connect more deeply to God. You know as you try something new, and are a success at it, you have the strength to act upon what you have imagined, and you see things becoming easier and better in your life. The universe wants you to be better organized so you can focus more completely on what connects you to the God of your own heart. You can rely on your intuition to lead the way and make the future bright. Trust and allow greater ease in your life so you can experience the fullness of God. Trust what is next; trust that it will bring about your highest and best.

Affirm: *I accept that right now is a vital new moment of time. I affirm that all negative attitudes are now dissolved, and I go free to live this day in an organized way. I know that I have everything in me to create an organized life and that such a life is possible. I trust that my best interests are always met* *with the highest and best for all involved. I am supported in conquering what-ever resistance is holding me back. Freedom is calling, and I'm listening as I make conscious choices that are steeped in love and not fear, as I plant seeds of faith and self-love, knowing that I am worthy of every organizing success.*

• • •

ACCEPTANCE

The first step toward change is awareness.
The second step is acceptance.
—Nathaniel Branden

Your opportunity as a spiritually evolving individual is to look at the conditions of your life and to accept your current state of af-fairs for what it is—a set of present-moment facts—nothing more and nothing less. You must reflect on the notion that you are a free and spiritual being with unlimited potential. An acceptance, without judgment, of what is, can move you to a greater expression of what is possible.

Accepting your current organizational issues doesn't mean ac-cepting that they are "inherently yours" or "can't be changed." You may want to hold on to the truth that what is "inherently yours" is the being hidden inside you and not what you see around you. Remember that any snag in life is a wake-up call to do and be some-thing that you desire to be. The occurrence of things that you don't like is not evidence that God doesn't love you. Accept that an unor-ganized experience is the manifestation of old beliefs. Know that the seeds you are now planting will bear a more organized way of life.

By accepting what is and moving on, you demonstrate the belief that your next step is going to be a lesson in how you can get closer and more connected to the God of your own heart. By trusting that the discomfort you feel is the harbinger of a teaching moment, that you have the power and the strength to shift your consciousness and align it with a more desirable result, your life will change. There are no more "excuses," no more turning to your story of how disorganized or late you always are. You must simply stop and accept that that version of your life story is utterly malleable; with one thought you can rewrite it. You are living just one thought away from the good that you desire. Just one thought away.

Given where you are right now and the knowledge that the power that lies within can move through any obstacle, miracles will abound. New manifestations will occur in your outer experience—a lifestyle marked by a greater sense of organization, health, wealth, and overall happiness is moving toward you. By quieting the inner critic and opening to your inner well of support, you experience a shift in perception, attitude, and ultimately in your experience. Your goals, dreams, and desires manifest. Your life becomes happier from the inside out because you have stopped surrendering to circumstance.

Organizing can be a lot of work, a lot of physical stuff to manage and a lot of mental work to sort what we own and decide what we need, how to store it, and the like. You can easily be overwhelmed. "Where to begin? What needs to be done? How am I ever going to do this?" can stop you right at the beginning. That is why it is critical to have not only the inner desire to get to the other side but to have faith in your abilities to manage the journey. Accept what is, it is no big deal. Shake those pearly gates, call on the heavens to help, and drop into the brilliant intuition that is lying beneath the surface of your busy mind.

* * *

Contemplation: Inner Stillness

I quiet my mind and open my heart.
I breathe in and out several times.
All is quiet and all is well.

In a moment of worry, I find that locating my pulse moves me into the space where I feel the sacredness of just being alive. It can be that simple. Take a moment, take a deep breath, and relax until you feel the power of the Spirit within yourself. Focus on it, get to know it, see it as a friend, and form a relationship with it. Your connection to that source is your ticket out of a disorganized environment. Putting up photos of organized places, creating a vision board of pictures of serenity on your fridge or on your workspace filing cabinets, can be great ways to trigger the mind to move back to positive thoughts of what you're capable of. When you slow down to be centered in your connection to the divine good, you feel powerful and able to take on any organizing task.

Affirm: *There is a great sense of power that dwells within me. As God's beloved, I'm free to overlook past mistakes and regrets and move forward in peace. This truth allows me the freedom to move forward on an organized path, one that is mine alone. I'm open to this and allow this awareness to help me when I'm starting to get organized. My mindful, calm self allows for all the good to enter. I am successful in this process.*

• • •

In *Part II – Your Mind*, we explored the power of your beliefs and feelings, how the boundless creativity of the universe is at your disposal to help you in any activity you engage in, and how your positive thoughts about organization are made manifest by the action of metaphysical laws. We also examined the value your personal intuition has to your organizational process and how old resistance to moving toward an organized life can be overcome. Lastly, we considered how simply accepting things as they are, as your new starting point, is important to your success.

Old negative feelings of fear and lack of trust are likely to arise for you. Rather than simply ignore them, I urge you to embrace what they're showing you, so you can consciously turn them around. Your freedom starts from within; that is where all your power lies. Get still and listen to the voice inside, act on it and witness your life transformed.

PART III

YOUR TIME

Adopt the pace of nature.
—RALPH WALDO EMERSON

How you relate to time is a key factor in determining the quality of life you will experience. Many people, particularly those residing in the Western world, are challenged by their relationship with time. Our crazy, self-imposed schedules, where work never seems to go away and we are always chasing the clock, result in a chronic feeling of unhappiness. Combine that with modern technology, which has enabled people to be in many places at once and to engage in business at a dizzying pace. We are always doing something, always working as if our electronic communication has no time boundaries. This creates a false reality. Staying busy is perceived as a sign of self-worth and importance. However, when you feel that time is not your ally it causes you a lot of stress and uncertainty. You are always running but never getting anywhere.

Time is downright perplexing. We need it. Yet it doesn't truly exist. You tend to believe that there is such a thing as time, that it isn't an idea but a thing for you to control and manipulate. You tend to block time's flow and blame time for many of your troubles as you see the universe not as an eternity but in structured divisions. Time has been used to simply calculate your experiences and give you concrete measurements of your "wins" and "losses." The journey of your life is more than a simple Gregorian calendar system acknowledging the routines of your days. You have within yourself a much greater ability to influence your understanding and experience of time than you probably think.

For the most part, when you are not using your time to make money, you're using your time to spend money. Why is that so? It seems that most people are on automatic pilot as they go through life—always catching or resisting time, never in balance. It is ironic that the only way many people attempt to redeem themselves and feel connected is to spend money to take away the disjointedness of their day. As soon as they have some money (or even before), they spend it in an effort to feel better. Maybe they choose to buy new shoes or a new iPhone or get their bathroom remodeled; maybe they choose to go to the movies or out to lunch, but they frequently spend money in an effort to make themselves happy. (And they wonder why they have so many "stuff" issues!) Rather than be in the quiet of the moment, they seek distraction, a way to "pass the time." "Critical and urgent" activities that take up most people's time are in fact a tremendous waste. When was the last time you sat at a bus stop and just waited for the bus? Not looking at your device, not calling some-one to chat, just waited for the bus? If you're like most people, you refuse to have even a moment of "unfilled" time. This is a modern epidemic!! But this perpetual need to fill time actually robs you of your peace of mind.

Naturally, your perception of time is rooted in your ideas of real-ity—when you remove time from the mind, it stops. It is important for your general day-to-day experience that you have the right at-titude toward time and that you move through it in a peaceful way, knowing that there is plenty of it. Your interpretation of time also influences your biology. "How can that be?" you say! What do the words *weekday* and *weekend* mean to you? How does your physical body respond to them? Notice how one word or the other can shift the way you feel.

When you take a few seconds to consider how you use time and how you are invariably attempting to relieve the stress of your life, the tendency is to look to the physical for answers. All answers, however, are to be found inside. As I've laid out earlier in this book, you create the life you have. There is always a payoff for what you do. When I run into a person who is flustered and says, "I don't have time to talk," or "I'm just so busy," their perception is very telling. They feel that they're projecting an image of being important and on a superficial level, they are. But on a deeper level, what they're demonstrating is what they value and who they are.

I used to lecture to business executives, and during that phase of my career I, too, used an "old" version of time. I would talk about things such as productivity and time management and how to accomplish more by doing less. I always shared the latest calendar and daily list apps that would help measure and divide the endless cycle of the days. They helped my clients and me feel more in control, or so I thought. I believed if you controlled time and micromanaged it, you would feel better at the end of day. I've since come to believe that getting more done isn't the way. Rather, the better approach is to first know that you have more than enough time to do what needs to be done and second, attend to the right things. When it comes to achievements, at the end of the day quality is more important than quantity. There is always going to be a list.

Instead of managing time, I would argue that you should start to manage your state of mind and the thoughts and opinions that you have of time. The notions of the past and future are concepts that you want to move beyond; you see time very differently when you realize that there is only the eternal moment. You should always remember that time is an abstract human concept. Einstein changed the world's concept of time with his theory of relativity, showing that time can be stretched and twisted, like saltwater taffy. By pushing yourself to rise above the everyday human understanding of time and allowing yourself to luxuriate in the "endless moment," you can be at greater peace.

And you can employ that peace in getting and staying organized.

If you're rushing or hurrying, the thoughts behind those activities are based in fear that you'll "run out" of time. As you continue to rush, you become increasingly less in sync with your center, and as your thoughts are always creating reality, they will attract a physical reality of chaos and the further need to rush. This is how the law of attraction works; it will create more situations that cause you to rush and hurry and feel unsettled. When you feel this type of situation arise, you must stop what you're doing, slow down and move off that "frenetic" frequency.

Rather than always asking yourself, "What is the best use of my time?", I suggest asking, "How can I connect to my source and be more present than absent? What is the one thing that I can do right now to be in a deeper conversation with the Spirit?" Going to God, not your calendar, for inspiration is the way to feel free, alive, and capable of accomplishing what needs to get done. If you operated throughout the day with this desire and could truly live in what you were experiencing, time would stand still; and you would feel an expansiveness in which you feel whole, complete, and perfect with what is happening. Perhaps you just completed a yoga class or came back from a mediation retreat or spent some time in nature. Often, time in these different contexts generates the same feelings of spaciousness, joy, and peace.

Being present and being aware of what you are feeling in any given moment is where true freedom is. When time stops, the mind stops—the thinker isn't busy thinking but being. This is a place of great empowerment, where the entire being takes a moment to be still and connect. You've no doubt heard it a million times, and yet you continue to ceaselessly try to control time. Time is where the ego lives—the stronger your connection to your ego, the better able it is to bully you and the less freedom you may have. Time isn't your source – God is.

It requires deep thought to remember that there is no time in the mind of God and to understand the timelessness of the spiritual essence of your being. We are all eternal beings in consciousness. As Ralph Waldo Emerson said, "Consciousness is the only reality," and it is at the center of your being. You don't live in the past or in the future; you live right now in this one moment of time. It is a gift to yourself to live with this insight and to allow life to flow more freely all around you, with your new organized life furthering your peace of mind.

You must trust that your experiences are in order. Divine flow is all around you, and your desires for organizing come from a higher sense of purpose in your life. When you live in the divine flow, insights or answers appear from the truth that ultimately guides you. For example, a person who has a calm and nonreactive mind is filled with awareness of the infinite, where there is no place for anxiety or any kind of urgency. An individual with a calm and centered mind cannot be misled into creating organizing systems that don't support him or her.

The creative process that responds to your thoughts knows time only as now, just as it knows only one place—here. This is why, in declaring where you're headed and what your plans are for the day, it is most effective to describe your destination as though you already occupy it, as though you own it. You mustn't forget that there is only one time, and try not to be concerned about things happening at the "right" time. You can create a new relationship with time if you look at it differently. Rather than feeling that time is a scarce commodity, affirm that you have all the time you need to complete everything that needs to get done.

What you're experiencing today has come to you from a collection of all the present moments you've lived through. Being in a state of flux or movement is an opportunity for you to create a new path, to let go of what is and see what is possible. What makes life a real challenge is when you're dwelling in a time that isn't now: concerned with yesterday or worried about tomorrow. Being in the moment, you're in balance, with a greater sense of ease and being in the flow.

The next time you're waiting for the bus to arrive (or better yet, when you feel like you have a million things to do!), seize that time and imagine that your desires come to fruition; you arrive on time and all gets done! You can, and should, do this with great frequency. When you're driving and waiting for the light to change, or in line at the grocery store, chill out. Breathe and feel grateful for the extra time. Change your attitude and use this as a meditation time. Your job is to bring light, possibility, and hope into every challenging situation you encounter.

And just to be clear, this type of thinking, envisioning a day that is peaceful and productive, is not at all the same type of thinking about the future that most people engage in. This is setting the universal forces ahead of you in everything you do and everywhere you go, for a positive experience; it is not worrying about the traffic or whether your supervisor will become snarky when you ask for a week off. Envision a happy series of outcomes; and then, do one thing at a time. (Being fully present to the task at hand.)

The work you do to get organized and become connected to your truth is meant to invite divine order into your life today. Thinking about consequences is particularly important when you're considering bringing yet another object, expense, or time commitment into your life. Remember that being organized is about making your life easier, but the reverse is also true: the simpler you make your life, the easier it is to stay organized.

In the upcoming chapters, I will examine how important it is to understand the eternal moment. The ultimate goal isn't just to get organized but to give your full attention to what you are doing in the moment. Finding your own personal rhythm is one of the best ways to deal with stress. I'll discuss living with the mantra of timelessness (peace with time) rather than focusing on lack of enough time to get organized. You'll see how your understanding of the fluidity of time leads to slowing down, to resting in the wisdom of oneness, and to creating an organized life. You will discover that you have all the time you need when you stop measuring it and controlling it. Be in the present moment—the place where peace is felt.

CHAPTER SEVEN
THE ETERNAL MOMENT

The time is now; the place is where we are,
and it is done unto us, as we believe.
—ERNEST HOLMES

I f you're honest with yourself, you probably spend a lot of time
feeling like you should be someplace other than where you are at
that moment. How often I've been in the middle of something
only to wish it to be done and over with and then when I think back
to that experience, I can remember very little about it. It seems to
be human nature to want to feel good right now and to always be
searching for a quick fix to make it happen.

When you decide to dance with the divine and cultivate a practice to experience the truth of who you are, you learn to appreciate
the eternal moment, the place where time stops. Since most people
equate "being in motion" with being successful or important, they
do not value the benefits of slowing down to experience the present

moment. The present moment, in which you can connect to the eternal presence of God, is where you find the source that guides you throughout your life. When you want to get organized, you can see how your worries and concerns about time management really contribute to your challenges, and unfortunately, you may tend to give up.

Do you live to work, rather than to be? The best things for you don't demand you to be in a hurry, anxious, and panic stricken. Remember that speed kills. Another problem is that you feel like you need to do everything all at once, be busy all the time, every single moment that you're awake. I am constantly hearing the complaint that there isn't enough time! Time, however, did not get lost, and it doesn't need to be found. You don't need to control time but rather be at peace with it. Playing "beat the clock" isn't the goal of life.

I urge you to examine another way to look at time, a place where oneness and harmony lead your life; a place where inner peace and deep connection to all is made possible by the expansiveness of the Spirit. Since peace can only be found in the present moment, it becomes your duty to be present, learning to ignore cravings and desires that live outside of you. I know that if my day is highly structured and marked by checking things off my mental list, I will be going against my natural flow. I'll feel out of step, anxious, and worried.

You are the winner if you're willing to reduce what is extra and unnecessary in your daily life, like your current stuff and your desire to have more stuff, and to increase the positive power that resides within you. The false, unhappy self that is cluttered and constantly behind comes as a result of living from the outside not the inside. The benefits of doing less in a world that has embraced a "crazy running in circles to fulfill someone else's requirements" game, is that you'll have time to search for what truly will sustain you.

People generally look at time as linear, referring to a clock, a calendar, or a list of things to do. There is also natural time, reflecting the flow of life, such as the four seasons and the cycles of the sun and the moon. Spiritual, or infinite time, provides you with unlimited energy and resources. It is the wellspring for anyone who accesses his or her creativity. This "spiritual time" has an eternal quality; it doesn't feel like time is passing slowly, more like time does not exist at all.

How can you stay in this space as much as possible throughout your day? If you slip out of it, how can you get quickly back to that space? Practice by creating some space in your day. Try not to fill in every minute in your calendar or your head. See that life is a moment-to-moment experience, where you are mindful of time but not controlled by it. Let your natural instincts guide you such that you are not procrastinating but are not rushing either. I guarantee that you will be more peaceful and at ease. When time takes over your life, dysfunction and anxiety set in. Think about it. Time pressures are seldom the result of what's actually happening at any given moment. They are much more closely related to something that's already happened or what you project may happen.

Creating a new relationship with time from a different perspective can help you in your organized life. I encourage you to embrace time, affirm that you have all the time you need to do everything you want to do, and you will. Various branches of science see time as if it were infinite. The Buddhist perspective of time is the essence of emptiness. What does time mean to you?

You want to learn to trust that your moment-by-moment experience is fulfilling and giving you enough direction. If you can eliminate nonproductive tasks and mindfully move through your day in a peaceful way (that doesn't have to be linear or sequential), you can make the most of things. I recognize that you likely have a job that requires you to work for a set number of hours, and that you might have other responsibilities that are scheduled for certain times of the day. You can, however, in spite of such commitments, make a point of having an internal sense of calm and holding on to it regardless of what is going on around you. The urgency of your daily life is created, and can therefore be dismantled, from within.

Honestly examining your relationship to time and understanding how to find ways to rejuvenate and lead an intentional life, will create a physical world that will reflect just that. There is nothing that is going to give you more peace and everlasting joy than to be honest about what fulfills you and you alone. Take the time to find what that is and to create a life in which the experience of each moment reflects your desires.

* * *

ONENESS

A hectic schedule crammed with nonpurposeful activities
precludes an experience of inspiration.
—Wayne Dyer

The daily, incessant busyness of your life decides the direction and quality of your existence and either pulls you to an outward experience or an inward experience. People typically adapt to an increasingly faster tempo that keeps them feeling important but rarely leaves them with a sense of accomplishment at the end of the day. There is nothing wrong with setting goals, striving for achievements, and checking things off a list. That is all fine. However, it becomes a problem when you never feel like you are getting enough done and are on a constant search for connecting with something externally rather than internally.

There is just one moment in your life when deadlines and duties don't exist, when you believe you have more time than ever and when there are no past regrets or worry about the future. That moment is now. When I allude to the power of this moment, I'm referring to the power of living connected to the one life that is all around you, feeling the power of the divine good liberating you from active, busy, and worldly thoughts. By not seeking refuge in the outer world, you can approach your day in a different way and bring the oneness of life to the forefront.

By tapping into the timelessness that is, you can be in the world but not ruled by it. Coming to peace with the consciousness that brought you to your state of current organizational woes cannot take you any further. The accumulation of belongings is not what ultimately sustains you and gives you what you are longing for. (You know it!) When you realize that the problem is fixable and you are able to turn your attention inward and connect to your oneness with the divine and infinite source, a new way of creating order will arise for you. A subtle but consistent shift in awareness is the grease behind the wheel.

Turning toward the infinite source will provide the answer. Before you know what the answer is, you call up the feeling of already knowing the answer, the feeling of peace, wholeness, and harmony—whatever seems to meet the situation. (This goes far deeper than just saying some affirming words, as the thought that powers your words cannot be denied.) Those two glorious things are the most profound springboards for accomplishing more of what really matters.

By giving your full attention to the oneness of all life, to all experiences, an intelligence far greater than the ego manifests in your life. Your natural state is to feel oneness with your innermost self.

What is essential is your connection to the power within that can dissolve past failures and negative thoughts about what it takes to get organized and to make that transition easy and successful.

When you start to get organized or even to think about it, be as present as you can, as the past cannot take hold of you while you are reaching out to the fullness of what you are capable of. When your attention goes to the past and reaffirms those stories of being unsuccessful at getting organized, take a deep breath and come back to the present moment. When you root in the stillness of your being, tapping into the sacredness of life that is within, you will be rooted in possibility. That is how it all begins. That is how you change your organizing situation.

If you wait for "the right time" or "the right thing" that it takes to become organized, success will elude you. You don't need to find that impossible extra week off from work to do it. When you slow down, so does time, and that is why you can experience an abundance of time to complete your organizing tasks. Calmly knowing and being aware that you set the tempo of your experience, you can continually practice being in the now, bringing a timeless dimension to what you do.

The more conscious you become of your key stressors and the unproductive habits you've developed in regard to time, the closer you'll be to freeing yourself from their net. Encourage yourself to have little periods when you can connect to nothing but the present. You don't have to sit on a cushion or recite sacred texts. Rather, you can go for a walk on your coffee break at work or just sit on a park bench and be a witness to life that is moving all around you. You can fit the practice into any time of day. By developing a new perspective of time, your relationship to it will change.

Because creative thoughts are nonlinear, I encourage you to

draw a circle, which reflects the eternal now, and to write all your activities inside that circle. Remember that there is no beginning or end to a circle; it contains only the eternal present moment. It also reflects when humanity and divinity unite; the expression of the Spirit in form. Be one with the Spirit, and you will transcend whichever overly human ideas about time are limiting to you.

* * *

Contemplation: Transcendence

I quiet my mind and open my heart.
I breathe in and out several times.
All is quiet and all is well.

As you enter into a realization of your connection with the Spirit, which is fully alive and well within you, you know that your spiritual progress and well-being are assured and that you can be successful at getting organized. You transcend material reality; you become right on track and manifest a calm and peaceful environment. By believing that everything happens *for* you, and not *to* you, you intentionally develop a servant heart, refining your life in service to all. You thereby transcend this world by acting from above.

Affirm: *Viewing time as my ally, I allow today's events to unfold according to an unlimited intelligence. I trust the intelligence to usher me into well-being, and I joyously claim the gifts of a new day. I awaken to the precious light of this new day and experience the oneness in all life.*

• • •

HARMONY

Happiness is not a matter of intensity,
but of balance, order, rhythm, and harmony.
—THOMAS MERTON

With the pace of life today, you may sometimes have a frantic feeling, like time is passing too quickly. You would like a deep feeling of balance and harmony in your life, in how you spend your day, and with the people you know. When you feel a sense of uneasiness, are nervous or anxious about trying new things, and lack faith that all is going well, having a schedule that doesn't drain you is a major benefit. Most people, and you're probably among them, equate activity with productivity and are addicted to busyness. These are big hurdles to overcome in your quest for a sense of harmony in your day.

There are many ways in which you can either discourage harmony with the choices you make throughout your day or seek peace and practice contemplation. Getting organized rarely makes it to the top of anyone's fun-to-do list. It is something you know you could improve upon, but you don't know where to begin. When you can't shake the feeling that you "should" be doing something "more productive," you're not likely to devote the time needed to turn within and find your peaceful center—you're much more likely to check Facebook, channel surf, and ultimately, imprison yourself with false beliefs about your inability to "manage" your time. Purge the frequent thought pattern that you must be tending to some outer task (or entertainment!) at all times. Take one step at a time, and you will begin to see results in your areas of disorganization and know that you are supported and guided in improving your life.

I'm aware that the practice of paying attention to your inner life *and* the world around you seems nearly impossible. Have you ever noticed that when you are in a hurry, you only think about getting there on time? Your focus is on what's wrong: you are late. When you aren't in a hurry, you focus in on what's right. Getting to a particular destination takes the same amount of time regardless of how you perceive it, but how the time is spent can be vastly different.

Eckhart Tolle claims, "Awareness is the power that is concealed within the present moment." (That is why it is sometimes referred to as presence.) How often have I been mindless about what I was doing? No matter where I was, I needed to be somewhere else. I was everywhere but in the moment. My body was in one place, but my mind was elsewhere. To find an increase in balance and harmony between the repetitions of your daily routines, seek out some time, however brief, to explore and connect to the silence within. The constant connection to your divine source is what makes the daily journey sacred.

There is something within you that stirs your heart and makes you want to connect with others. When your mind isn't pulled by endless false desires, you can then take every step, fresh, alive, and aware. When your activities mirror the ease within your mind, and you're creating systems that nourish your soul, peace is at the door. Remind yourself that harmony is how peace presents itself and that peace can only exist in the present moment. What you seek, seeks you, and you draw into your life what you need to create wholeness, harmony, and ultimately, peace.

Unfortunately, many people allow the things they most dislike to do, or to have, succeed in taking up the majority of their mental time. When society's version of clock time obscures your natural rhythm, the ease you seek in your day is easily lost. Adopt a strategy of living by your own rhythm, and find the essence of flexibility and freedom in how you go about your day. When you sense that your intuition is leading the way, happiness and harmony characterize your experience. To strengthen your vibrancy in life and develop greater freedom and joy, replace reacting with acting; you are the one deciding how you feel at any given moment.

. . .

Contemplation: The Art of Allowing

I quiet my mind and open my heart.
I breathe in and out several times.
All is quiet and all is well.

Make it a practice to spend your time looking through the eyes of unconditional acceptance, seeing what is right about others and yourself. The Spirit within guides you in easily balancing your life. It's all about choice. Freedom comes from reminding yourself that in every single moment you get to choose which path to take. Listening to your own inner wisdom, you can decide to use the courage residing within you, which brings you to your highest good. Peace, joy, and harmony are calling to you this very minute, luring you back to the beauty that life has to offer.

Affirm: *I have no regrets about the past. I live this moment fully and in the joy of God. Clock time is artificial, and time itself is infinite. The eternal now is the only moment in which I can live. I am relaxed and peaceful in it. God never hurries. God's time is my time. It is always sufficient for my needs. I use it in an orderly manner.*

CHAPTER EIGHT

A CONNECTION
TO THE PRESENT

There is no greater obstacle to God than time.
—MEISTER ECKHART

I t is hard to receive answers, or to even feel justified resting at the end of the day, when your external world controls your internal experience. When you waste your time on your variety of modern-day electronic busyness, or run around doing errands that keep you distracted and focused on the external, you move further from the deep presence that dwells within. The nonstop digital influx is tiring, and if you're like most Americans, it's using up every spare moment you have. Although you use your devices in order to "stay connected," most people will tell you that their online communications make up for much of their daily activities.

Engaging in hours of social media interchanges may be a way to experience the values of today's society, but when the day is over, you don't feel very satisfied. What's remarkable is how quietly addictive these activities are. Before you know it, you're back in front of the screen "liking" someone's snapshots of her weekend at the shore and matching celebrities with their baby photos and getting up at 3 a.m. just in case you missed something. If you haven't succumbed to the seduction of the screen, you're overwhelmingly busy—working, shopping, driving your kids around—even going to a yoga class becomes one more item on the to-do list. Being busy (and of course, multitasking) is both "demanded" by your schedule and applauded by our society. You're constantly compelled onward to the next thing, mistaking activity for accomplishment, or as John Wooden would say, "Don't mistake activity with achievement."

If you're like most people, you cannot bear the quietness and the stillness that is the present moment—you're much more comfortable dwelling in the pursuit of immediate gratification (the "shop now and think later" attitude that is so prevalent today). It is so much easier to stuff yourself with whatever distracts you than it is to be alone with yourself. You live in a culture of motion, a culture of becoming and seeking but never arriving at one's deep and desired expansion, never experiencing the connection to the silence of one's heart.

Although your true nature is beyond worldly time, you nonetheless feel uncomfortably out of balance when you haven't done what you thought you needed to do on any given day. To mitigate your feelings of distress about this, you naturally start to run harder, but not smarter. You wind up "stealing" time, rather than actually getting more. The constant stimulation of entertainment and information distracts you from turning inward, and by devoting every spare moment toward this new nonstop digital world, you're left feeling tired and on edge. You find it hard to stay centered, to be mindful of what is true at the core of your being.

There are now one billion websites and over 1.55 billion users on Facebook. A third of the American workforce feels that they have little time to actually focus on and process the work they do, and over half feel they are so distracted that they find it hard to get their real work done. Six million Americans have a hard time sleeping at night—and their anxiety about getting it all done *now* robs them of a peaceful, and mindful, life. Workers report that they are constantly switching from task to task, spending an average of three minutes on a particular task before moving to another, and researchers find that an average of two hours a day is spent "recovering" from distractions. Not only are you robbing yourself of a most precious gift but you're also reinforcing the idea for future generations that multitasking and busyness are the accepted way of being. The risk is that they too will fail to access a healthy inner dialogue and to learn that time engaged in real self-care is the most rewarding way to spend their time.

What people really yearn for is a deep connection to their present. This experience requires your focus; when you take the time to reflect upon who you are, you change both your own future and that of those around you. To better focus on your inner self and your divinity, you should remind yourself that time is an illusion. What is missing isn't an abundance of time but rather your attention to what you are doing in the moment. It is one of the few things that have a truly calming effect and assure us that we're right where we need to be.

Remind yourself often that your true nature transcends time. When you don't recognize this essential truth, it is easy to feel overwhelmed, unable to complete your daily tasks. But think about how you feel about your day when you go to bed at night. Do you look back with satisfaction on all the things you crossed off your list? Would it not feel more rewarding to have achieved just a little stronger connection with your higher self? When you look back upon your life with an open heart, you will see that your most fulfilling achievements were driven by passion and empathy, not by the completion of a list of tasks.

As you let go of your smaller self in favor of your higher self, your relationship to time changes. You might say the smaller self lives in worldly time, and the higher self lives in ethereal time. It is important that you measure the quality of your life by the extent to which your inner goals are brought to the surface and not by how busy you are. It is said that when Gandhi became too busy in the outside world, he would repeatedly utter the words "Ram, Ram, Ram," in order to return back to his divine self. This practice helped to locate his peaceful core; it can also help you to be guided and rested in the present.

• • •

GUIDANCE

There is guidance for each of us, and by slowly listening we shall hear the right word...Place yourself in the middle of the stream of power and wisdom, which animates all whom it floats, and you are without effort impelled to truth, to right and to perfect contentment.
—RALPH WALDO EMERSON

Time is an illusion. The guidance you need to be present with yourself is available to you at all moments. How ironic that the only thing that can save you from the tyranny of worldly time is the power of the present moment, where "stillness speaks" and guides you into your greater experience. Remember that you are not in the past, and you are not in the future. You are here now. Everyone has the ability to step back from the demands on their day, to evaluate them dispassionately and to respond intelligently to what goes on around them rather than just blindly reacting to them. By taking the time to plot the road that you're on, clearer paths will emerge for you. You receive answers from the heavens, not from the confines of your calendar app in which you've allocated no time for self-exploration.

As American author Wayne Muller points out: "In our spiritual life we need to listen to the God who constantly speaks, but whom we seldom hear in our hurried deafness." If you were able to concentrate, focus, and seek out simplicity when making decisions, you would find that the laws of the universe are easily apparent, and your actions are in alignment with the divine plan. For organizing purposes, the gift is the ability to listen to your intuition for guidance and work from your intentions, thereby creating a lifestyle that truly feeds your soul. I suggest (and yes, this is a typical organizing idea, but bear with me) simplifying your life. If you remove from your day as many things that require your attention as possible, you're on your way to controlling your daily experience.

How can you be a mystic in the everyday world? How do you bring God into all your activities? Can you imagine how much more enjoyable the process of goal attainment would be, how much more dynamic your experiences would be, if they were infused with a God-quality? When I need guidance about how I'm going to succeed at organizing, I focus my attention on God, turning my mind away from the actual problem and centering my thoughts on the divine. I meditate on the qualities of the Spirit such as organizing, beauty, and peace.

Bringing the essence of God into your consciousness is a fundamental practice of New Thought philosophy. My version of spiritual time management is about how "I serve God" and what qualities of God I bring forth, not about how much I acquire or how much I get done. Perhaps the only thing to acquire is a loving and open heart that is connected to your divine flow of goodness. A spiritual look at time management counteracts compulsive behavior that stems from compulsive thinking—thinking that is really a result of your feelings of separation from the divine.

Ernest Holmes suggests that you can be in an intimate relationship with the Spirit in all that you do throughout the day by letting go of what is not true, such as fear, worry, and the like, and focusing on elements of the divine. Do you live in regret (the past) or hope (the future)? Do your thoughts fluctuate between the two? If you feel exhausted more often than you like, ask yourself if your mind tends to dwell in the past and or on the future. Attachment to the past and stressing about the future just wears you down and makes it a challenge to become organized.

Tolle makes an insightful distinction between "clock time" (a phrase I used earlier referring to dealing with practical things) and "psychological time" (identification with the past or projection into the future). He suggests that you suffer when you allow psychological time to control your life, and by dwelling there, you miss being in the now. Now is the place where you have access to the true guidance of the divine—where you attract everything that you require. Although many phrases in our culture suggest that time is our enemy—time crunch, time constraints, killing time, working against the clock—as I said earlier, time is not your enemy. Choose to make time your ally, and choose to make it work for you. Practice taking time, or making time, for the things that are most important to you. It's easy to let time take control of you, but it's wonderful to learn the secrets of taking control of time. You will discover the expansive relationship you have with time when you stop measuring time in fifteen-minute increments.

Everything seems to be subject to time, yet we never experience time itself. We only experience what happens in the present moment. As Tolle said, "Time is the horizontal dimension of life, the surface layer of reality. Then there is the vertical dimension of depth, accessible only through the portal of the present moment." So, make an attempt to strip off the layer of time from your consciousness. In a way, it is the same as stripping off your ego. The ego needs you to take out the present moment and put you in the past or the future. Of course, attachment to the past and stressing about the future just wears you down; these mental activities are nothing but energy vacuums.

By shifting whatever false thinking you may engage in about time and how it holds you back, you can then connect the dots and find synchronicity, flow, and ease. Guidance will come to you in the eternal, silent moment. Try this exercise:

a) Write down all that you really desire your organized life to be like now.

b) Prioritize your organizing wish-list.

c) Pick the first item of your list, and write down the essence of what you desire (for example, feeling more organized).

d) Now write down any fear or thoughts you might have about not being able to manifest your organizing desire.

e) Flip the above statement to a positive, current expression, and use it as the basis for an affirmation.

* * *

Contemplation: Silence

I quiet my mind and open my heart.
I breathe in and out several times.
All is quiet and all is well.

Try experiencing silence. Focus on your breath, an object, or a concept, anything that anchors your ever-changing, moody mind. If you are receptive to physical activities, then try yoga or tai chi. Spend time creating a clearer pathway to God, and your conversation with the divine will become louder. By seeking the peace of being in the present, you find that you're fully satisfied and need nothing external to feed you or give you a better experience.

Affirm: *I quiet my mind and reconnect to the Spirit. I take a few deep breaths; and then, I listen. What does my inner guidance lead me to see, hear, or know? I awaken to new feelings and deeper awareness as I experience greater calm and move forward in confidence, knowing that I am guided in the right direction. My mind is aligned with a deeper essence that helps me organize my thoughts. I seek out and ask for what will uplift my soul. I know that my intentions are heard and all is well.*

• • •

RESTING

There are greater rhythms, seasons and hormonal cycles and sunsets and moonrises and great movements of seas and stars. We are part of the creation story, subject to all its laws and rhythms.
—WAYNE MULLER

Because you're human, you live in a world of duality with respect to time – your time and God's time. The former is filled with your day-to-day momentary desires (hunger) and responses to what happens to you (a text on your phone). These events keep you in motion, constantly trying to avoid discomfort. They tug at your ego, which doesn't want you to be at peace and doesn't want you to take the time required to be more organized. A new life in the present moment would diminish the ego, and so the ego objects mightily to your efforts to know yourself. What we deeply seek is a place where we can transcend the earthly realm and enter into Milky Way-galaxy time, or, as Tolle would say, the enlightened ones will still exist in clock time but are free of psychological time.

According to the Buddhists, the only way to feel truly rested is to be engaged in what actually needs to get done in the present moment and no more. In today's society, resting and slowing yourself down so as to be fully present in the moment is really hard to do. You are either seen as being weak or in desperate need to repair yourself. You can benefit greatly by the use of simple mantras to live more fully in the present and to connect to a feeling of timelessness. A life of mindful prayer will keep you centered and stable and will allow you to live from the heart rather than only from the head. In this quiet union with the Spirit, you can recognize your true self and claim a life that is balanced, organized, and in perfect harmony.

In the moment, the now, the present, most earthly problems disappear, as your ego is not at the forefront, assaulting you with memories and anticipation. In the now, you become reenergized and open to new possibilities in your life. This subtle shift of consciousness is where the new connections are made and where the right things to be done are revealed. Accordingly, your productivity increases, and you become calm and deliberate in your actions. This can lead to feeling happy, as your day is passed with a sense of peace and accomplishment.

The word "Sabbath" means a time of rest, and traditionally the Sabbath is also a time of remembering that everything one has is a blessing. If you can be more present than absent in the day-to-day duties of your life, you can get your tasks accomplished and yet still stay connected and conscious of the eternal now that is in each moment. Everyone needs the opportunity for renewal. If you do not rest, you lose your way and your purpose. In truth, the real work is always done in the silence of your soul, right now, in the present moment. I like to call it the calm way, when you are focused totally on what is at hand and are totally satisfied by your efforts.

Try to take every opportunity you can to step off the treadmill of daily tasks and take a breather. Fill yourself with the awareness of your inner divinity. By being focused and mindful, you can enter the space the mystics call grace, in which you are renewed. Author Joel Goldsmith once said, "We are never alone and we know it. This sweet presence gives us an inner rest; it enables us to relax from the strain of the world and brings us joy and peace." Your higher self isn't attached to the trappings of minutes ticking by; you can free yourself from the obsessive *doing* that life seems to ask of you.

In your morning meditation, you can gently fall into the feeling that there is always enough time and allow yourself to slip into the sense of timelessness. There is in fact a great abundance of time. Start to shift your understanding, and rejoice in the ease that comes with all the time you need. Remember that this very moment offers a doorway to a new way of existing in the world, calming your mind and healing your heart. The only area of organization that you can shift and heal is available now in this moment. By ending the false sense of time that is ruling your life, the present takes on an expansive, rather than a restrictive quality. I've asked myself many times as I go to bed, "What brought me joy today?", and the answers surprise me. They are never what I would have expected.

Like your limited thinking about the nature of time, you have the ability to free yourself from wrong notions about your poorly organized life. Let the past actually stay in the past. It got you here to this moment; allow it to dissipate from your mind and to change what is. Rethink how you hold the notion of time and rest in the presence throughout your day. You will get much more done. Try some of these practices to jump-start your move in the direction and operating from your divine self:

a) *Turn toward peace*: Ask yourself, "Is this moving me in the direction of peace?" You have more than enough time in which to do everything when the present moment is your friend.

b) *Notice your breath*: Stay aware of the present moment by noticing your inhalation. Feel yourself smile inside. Notice your exhalation. Feel yourself smile. Repeat. Listen to whatever sounds are going on around you. Do you hear a coworker typing? Is a squirrel walking on the roof? Take notice.

c) *Attend to the most valuable task*: Ask yourself, "What is the most valuable thing that needs to be done in this moment?" Provide a specific answer. Perhaps it is a small step toward the goals or priorities that you've set for yourself. If so, take a moment to affirm that the goals are realistic and achievable.

d) *Appreciate one day at a time*: Most people have long-term goals when it comes to organizing, and while that is certainly the result you want, don't ignore the value of each step. Make a point of appreciating each achievement. Doing so will help bring you peace and yet motivate you to continue.

* * *

Contemplation: Congratulate Yourself

I quiet my mind and open my heart.
I breathe in and out several times.
All is quiet and all is well.

117

Congratulate yourself on your success in shifting the experience of time in your life. The awareness of time's expansiveness allows you to enjoy quiet periods throughout your day in which to rest in the arms of the Spirit. There you are nurtured and placed in a reality where you're able to connect to the bigger possibility that is your true self. Choose to make time your ally, and practice taking time and making time for the things that are important to you. Time is not your enemy. Celebrate your friendship with time and know that as you embrace an expanded notion of time, you will be helped and supported in getting your life organized.

Affirm: *I have more than enough time. I rely on the presence of God within me. Seeking wisdom and direction from the Spirit within me, I use the power that is within to shift my external circumstances and give my life the freedom and joy of becoming an organized person.*

CHAPTER NINE
SPIRITUAL
TIME MANAGEMENT

*When consciousness frees itself from its identification with
physical and mental forms, it becomes what we may call pure
or enlightened consciousness, or presence.*
—ECKHART TOLLE

How to extract more from one's time is a national obsession. The tendency is to adopt an increasingly faster tempo, when what you should do is the exact opposite—slow down, step off the treadmill, and take a breather. Because you have all the time you need, simply perceiving more of it makes way for the right things to get done. How you structure your day, and how you feel at the end of the day, are elements of spiritual time management; they matter a great deal to the quality of both your personal and professional lives.

The dominant organizing ideology stresses getting more done in less time, and the ego will let you keep chasing that goal until you either burn out or get sick. Being productive is important, but the constant doing, never getting a moment to yourself, will certainly damage your health and well-being. In spiritual time management, you learn to better manage your mind, and so the grip that traditional notions of time has on you is loosened—maybe even falls away altogether.

Your thoughts are born in the present moment, and when you have an awareness of residing in the present moment, your tendency to craft deliberate, positive thoughts is enhanced. You're then better able to dispel the ego and put forth joyfulness in each step that you take. In the present moment, the presence of the Spirit is available to you, and you're able to set powerful intentions in your various organizing strategies.

You must always come back to the notion that time is how you define it; time exists in your mind. Remember that you can't do anything about the past, including your own procrastination, so you might as well just move on. Ask yourself, what kind of tempo are you setting for your day? What are the stories that you tell yourself about time? What emotional layerings do you place on it? Do you need to feel and be busy to feel important? Do you also, or perhaps instead, tell yourself stories about why you "waste" time or why you're so often late for commitments? Do you complain about the lack of time because you find it less unnerving than settling into who you are beneath your ego-driven self?

Be a witness to your understanding of time. You don't need to be anywhere or do anything. Just be a witness to what you tell yourself about time, and with that, develop an understanding of how you can shift your thoughts about it and in turn, your usage of it. Your awareness is the seed of making a shift; it is ultimately the thing that gives you freedom. I once heard a New Thought minister say, "Whatever we think about, we bring about." This spiritual law, that the universe responds to what you put into it, plays an important role in how you manage your time.

Expectation is a powerful force for attraction, and intuition is a skill each one of us can access. When you use both, you can conquer any situation and manifest the life you want. If you can keep your eyes on the prize and visualize success, you'll start to feel it and see it take form in your life. What you focus on grows—so being stalwart in your expectations will result in their appearance in your life.

Certainly, linear time has a natural component. You experience it as the daily rising and setting of the sun and the changing of the seasons. You see it take shape as babies grow into children and then into adults. At another level, there is spiritual time, which, I believe, is eternal. In spiritual time, you are no longer enmeshed in traditional ways of feeling the passage of time, and you're connected more fully with that which is greater than you. Spiritual time provides you with unlimited energy, resources, and creativity; it is the realm in which you touch your non-ego-driven self, where the flow of expectation and action create a blessed experience.

During the years I worked as a corporate trainer, I tried many different ways to teach time-management strategies. One day I woke up with a new, inspiring, "God-centered" approach to time that liberates its users from the bondage of current time structures. No longer do you need to be checking things off your never-ending to-do list only to find out that you still have more to do. Enough already! I've found that a deeper and more fulfilling way to tackle your day is to look at time in a circular way; a way that incorporates the God essence of what speaks to your heart and lets that essence be part of all your actions. American author Thomas Moore observed, "All work on the soul takes the form of a circle, a *rotation*." I see the circle as representing all of what God is as well as where your earthly experiences take place. Rather than sending out energy in a straight (linear time) line, unify your forces with that of the Spirit. Get into the flow of your own energy and develop a sense of real purpose, a sense of completion. That will make you feel fulfilled and complete.

As you enter into spiritual time and as you become a more organized person, feel free to start and stop. Don't feel that if you haven't achieved something tangible that brings you closer to your goal every day, you've ruined your chance. Give up that kind of thinking! You are allowing yourself to become nonlinear, to move in the stream and the flow of the universal truth and see what magic appears in your life. Let go of the thoughts and behaviors that make you feel less-than. Explore, create new approaches, and allow yourself to have new feelings that transcend your everyday experience. Enjoy! I wish you oodles of time in which to play and to just veg out! Remember that "go" is no longer the only speed you have. Your new speeds can include "go," but they should also include "relax"—and you can (and will) feel so much more whole and happy!

As I've discussed, time usually feels like it is going in one direction, but in fact, it is a continual, ever-flowing circle of soul experience that doesn't have a start or finish. Spend time every day, perhaps after your morning meditation, while you have breakfast, or before you turn on your computer at work, and literally write down what essence you would like to experience in the actions that you undertake that day. By putting the being into doing, the Spirit knows what you want; it will deliver in a way that is the best for you. I am inviting you to completely change your thinking about time management, and if you are willing to do so, here are a few practices toward that end:

1. *Yesterday's Demonstration* - Examine one thing from the prior

day that brought more good into your life. Renew how you expressed that quality. Acknowledge the positive feeling and experience you had, and let the rest go. Reflect on this note when starting your new day, and take time to celebrate your demonstration. This is not about perfection but rather a willingness to express the Spirit.

2. *The God Quality* - Draw a large circle and create a smaller circle in the middle of that circle. Ask yourself what quality of God you'd like to embody today, and write that quality in the small circle. Have that quality serve as your anchor throughout the day—let it be the center of all of your actions. Some God qualities could be:

- Compassion
- Determination
- Intelligence
- Joy
- Kindness
- Love
- Passion
- Peace
- Personality
- Power
- Safety
- Stillness
- Trust
- Unity
- Wisdom

When you sit with that quality, ask yourself, "What must I release in order to express it most fully?" When you let go of certain thoughts or beliefs that hold you back, you become liberated and free from all personal, self-imposed restraints. For example, you decide that you want to experience joy in all of your actions, but you are anxious and worried or attached to an outcome. These feelings will prevent you from feeling that joy.

Make your to-do list for the day within the larger circle in the area that surrounds the God-quality circle. Limit yourself to no more than five tasks per day. Write down the more pressing ones first without any rigid structure. Let the Spirit guide you in creating a calendar that works for your highest self.

Enhance your success with the expression of the quality of God you select for the day by drawing an emblem, sketch, or pattern to represent it. Through your visual memory, it will deepen your experience.

Send your thoughts about your God quality out to the universe and believe that you are successfully bringing that quality into your day. Release any restraints you might impose on your experience of the quality.

3. *Affirmation* - When you affirm, you are carving out your higher good in the creative medium, so the experience you want to have is being brought forth. Your affirmation tells the universe what is true, and that truth echoes back to you as reality. Some affirmation examples follow: "Today is a fun day." "Life supports me." "The Spirit inspires me today." "I think thoughts of oneness today." *(Select one affirmation from the Appendix in the back of this book.)*

A spiritual time management plan is the place to take note of your mental intentions and how powerful they can be in shifting your organizational situation. By being more conscious of your relationship with the Spirit, you will find that you have more time in your day because you're doing the things that your higher self asks of you. You become relaxed, happy, and fulfilled. Bringing that God essence/quality to all of your various tasks and duties throughout the day serves to replace your more conventional, ego-driven experience.

As the Chinese philosopher Lao Tzu once said, "Just remain in the center [or circle], watching, and then forget that you are there."

Indigenous cultures use the symbol of the circle to represent eternity, the concept of no beginning and no end. The Religious Science circle represents God in its entirety (which would include the eternal now), and within that circle, a large "V" (going from top to bottom) represents the process through which thought is put into form, the infinite comes into being. When you unite the being with the doing, the mindful execution of the myriad of projects you undertake each and every day, there is satisfaction.

When I present this alternative approach to how to view time, people often express the concern that with this perspective they will not "get it all done." I understand that the attachment to mastering a daily to-do list can be pretty tenacious. Here's a technique I use to get past a challenge I might be creating in my mind: first, I take a few measured breaths and quiet my mind so that I'm open to receiving answers from within. I write down whatever is troubling me. (I like to do this in the morning as I start the day.) Second, I allow myself to feel whatever unpleasant feelings come to my awareness in connection with my perceived problem. I accept them and myself. I forgive myself for whatever issues I create. Third, I ask myself, "What lesson does this challenge want to teach me?" Fourth, I write down what I have learned about myself and my thought patterns and my ability to let go of any negative ideas I have.

Even if it bumps up against your "intellect," test the concept of "being" in spiritual time. You'll probably be surprised to find how productive you can be even when not watching the clock. Take note of the "coincidences" that arise that support your efforts—you'll begin to realize how well guided and cared for you are. Because your soul experiences time in a nonlinear way, why not offer it a nonlinear solution to time management? By focusing on a God quality that you wish to embody throughout your daily tasks, you're more attuned to the source that truly feeds you with energy and with wisdom. You feel more deeply and are enriched by knowing that the Spirit is flowing through you, guiding you through all of your undertakings.

In more conventional time management programs, you're urged to change those habits or activities that cause you to waste time and not feel good about yourself. I'm not going to tell you to refrain from changing such habits or activities because that wouldn't make any sense. On the other hand, such strategies alone don't work because they don't ask you to bring your awareness to the concept of how time flows in and out of your life. If you agree that what you lack is "clock time" (time on the outside), then it is time to look on the inside and acknowledge that staying busy is not a useful barometer to gauge how meaningful your life is.

$$\cdots$$

Slow Down

Distraction is married to discontent.
—Pema Chödrön

Time either works for you or it doesn't. One common experience that is particularly difficult for most people is the appropriate usage of time at work. Professional time issues are often connected to one's sense of duty and obligation. Traditional ideas about how to get more done in less time abound. What ideas do you hold about time in the workplace? How do you use it? Do you feel that your use of it is productive? If so, are you nurturing yourself as you go along, or is your use of time (albeit productive) also stressful? If you're living in America today, your already stressful life is compounded by your compulsion to multitask.

You undoubtedly "multitask" all day—even when you appear to be doing only one thing at a time, you're thinking of all the stuff that still needs to be done. Studies have shown that the multitasking that requires your mind to concentrate on more than one thing at a time is highly ineffective. Your brain simply can't tend to two things at once. I cannot urge you strongly enough to just try, for one entire day, to focus on one thing at a time. Don't rehearse the play in your head while you wait in line at the bank. Don't talk to your contractor on the phone while you skim through your emails. When the phone rings, turn around in your seat so that you're not facing your screen. Complete the phone call. Just do one thing. Allow yourself to be in a continuous flow by being conscious of the present moment.

Doing one thing at a time was the norm not all that long ago— our not-too-distant relatives practiced this simple approach to time management every day, focusing on the priorities that sustained them. The demands of your job and the abilities of technology have made it quite challenging to just be in the moment (or to stay there anyway), but I find that I'm much more productive (and at lot happier) when I focus on what I'm doing right now.

Another great way to diminish the stress in your life is to start consciously deciding *what* you will do *when*. You have the choice of whether you will be perpetually interrupted and distracted. Making decisions based on your preferences and inclinations allows you to be your best self. For example, I have a friend who likes to get up and work out before she starts her workday. She feels like it energizes her brain and helps her focus on what she wants to accomplish. Because you can't create more time, you need to create ways to maximize your use of it.

You should be mindful of the need for rest when scheduling your day—I know that I'm so much more productive from 8:00 a.m. until 2:00 p.m. than I am between 2:00 and 5:00, so I tend to schedule things that don't require much effort in the late afternoon. I work with my strengths. Check in with yourself throughout the day to learn your patterns. Knowing yourself, when your peak energies are or when you are better focused mentally, can help you set your course in the right direction. You can have a very good relationship with time when you generate deliberate and self-bolstering habits.

I don't just plan how I'll spend the day, but on Monday mornings I also develop a list for the week. I envision which tasks I most want and need to accomplish (which items I would be happy to have completed by Friday) and what might arise to deter me. I eliminate as many less-pressing tasks as I can (perhaps I can delegate them to someone else or do them at another time) and prepare a weekly (rather than a daily) list, as things can change so much in a day. When I strike them off the list, I can then see what I accomplished at the end of the week and feel really great about what I did.

When I don't take the time to plan (and to thus see the rewards), I feel less satisfied. Not having set a number of reasonably achievable goals, I'm more likely to obsess over what I didn't accomplish rather than what I did. This is typical. It's human nature to have a much stronger memory of what you failed at than of what you achieved. I may not be able to handle each paper only once, but I know that when I put my attention on what matters the most, the "A list," as I call it, it does get done and I'll be happy.

Sometimes I get rushed. I may have errands to run, deadlines to meet, and an overflowing to-do list. I hurry, believing I don't have time to get everything finished, and if something or someone gets in my way, I can easily lose my patience. I know that this race to the finish line is not a healthy or happy way to live, and yet I get caught in the busyness trap and forget that my outer life is generated by the image I hold inside. When I breathe and take a moment to rest and turn to my inner wisdom, I'm recharged in a much more centered (and yes, more productive!) way.

Wayne Muller said, "God does not want us to be exhausted; God wants us to be happy." It is important that as you realign your experience of time, you don't forget to take some time off. For some, this is the hardest part of adopting a spiritual approach to time management; however, you need your rest to connect with God and receive guidance to go in the right direction. Muller goes on to say, "Because we do not rest, we lose our way."

Slowing down is tough; it feels counterproductive to your ego-driven self. You have to encourage your inner self to get off the spinning hamster wheel in order to feel the fullness of spiritual time and to expand in that consciousness. Remember that all religious philosophies encourage people to stop, to feel and experience the endless quality of spiritual time. Through meditation you can drop out of the ever-churning thoughts and find the still center of your true being, where your awareness, centeredness, and mindfulness reside. I remind myself frequently that I am the one in control of my mind. Rather than let life overwhelm me, I stop, take a breath, and slow down. I remember that all things are working together in divine order. I can just as easily choose to be calm as I can to be anxious, so I choose calm. A sense of relief washes over me as I release the anxiety that caused me to be impatient. As I let go of my worry and hurry, I meet life's circumstances calmly and directly. I have all the time I need to complete whatever needs to be done. *This* is the practice.

Try a rhythm-time approach to your to-do list. I'm not advocating procrastination but rather a time of rest in order to refocus and renew your faith that your life is more than your daily accomplishments. Holmes said, "Rest in the perfect confidence, peace and certainty... never become anxious, never being hurried or worried." The central reason that you have what you don't want is because you think about what you don't want. Remember that when you focus on things that you don't want, such as "I don't want to be late," or "I don't want to be so disorganized," the law of attraction hears "be late," and "be disorganized." And so, the universe manifests exactly like that.

When you quiet yourself and your surroundings, you open yourself up to receive insights into what most needs to be done. This is a great technique for the workplace, as you can better understand the direction the company wants to take. When things around you aren't disturbing your tranquility, then you can hear. I recently learned about a company that is paying its employees to have a good night's sleep so they make fewer mistakes at work; sounds like a good policy to me!

Let's add another item to the list of things that weigh people down. I urge you to let go of the belief that feeling burned out and exhausted is the emotional mandate for the path to success. Are you acting from your most deliberate, highest self, or are you chasing the last thing that showed up in your in-box? When you can slow down, increase your attention span, and simply focus, you can change the pace of your busy life. The first step is to be still and go within. There is just one moment in life when workloads and deadlines don't exist, when you believe that you have all the time in the world, when there are no regrets about the past or concerns about the future—that moment is now.

Yes, today's workplace can be quite demanding. If your work environment is not one in which personal schedules are overtly accommodated, it is up to you to covertly arrange your time to suit yourself. There is no prize for being overworked, and your productivity will suffer if you're struggling. You must do your best under such circumstances to create a schedule that calms you and speaks to who you are.

* * *

Contemplation: Being in the Flow

I quiet my mind and open my heart.
I breathe in and out several times.
All is quiet and all is well.

When you are so in the moment that you lose yourself in that action, you are in the flow. When nonduality arises and you experience a deep soul connection to what you are doing, you are doing what you ought to be doing. These "mini-satoris,"—a "satori" is a Buddhist term for awakening or enlightenment—are the sweet nectar of life. It might be hard to imagine, but you can see organizing as a sacred, mindful practice that connects you to your greater self. When the outer self is reflecting what the inner self feels, you are in the flow of all that is right for you—not judging but being in the fullness that your heart desires. Connect the dots, observe the connections, and be grateful that you are open to all the divine goodness that is around you.

Affirm: *I restore my well-being by taking time to relax and feel the flow of Spirit all around me. As I relax and simply be by myself, I am at peace. As I bask in the stillness, I experience my eternal oneness with God and live in infinite peace in my life. I'm conscious and have made the right vibrational choice. I'm in the flow of life.*

• • •

DREAMS

...tomorrow is today's dream.
—KHALIL GIBRAN

You live in a world that's alive, creative, and ready to fulfill your dreams. Once you've accepted these notions, you can lead an intentional life, letting your conscious desires lead the way. But what about your subconscious desires? What about your daydreams and the thoughts you have when you're engaged in wishful thinking? In spiritual time management, your dreams play a critical supporting role. When you daydream about getting organized, what do you imagine? If you're reading this book, you may well be thinking that you would love to have room in your closet to hang up your favorite clothes, or that you'd like to actually arrive at the office *before* your supervisor tomorrow. The Swiss psychologist Carl Jung once said, "He who looks outside dreams, he who looks inside awakens." This idea is the spark that keeps you in the light and on the path to a greater, deeper experience of life.

Your conscious thoughts throughout the day plant the seeds of actions. But the moments between deliberate thought and conversations are the moments that really create your life. What you think is possible, what you think you can become, exists in these moments, when you're suspended from doing and can only be and dream. (Interestingly, you may already experience your daydreaming self in a sort of nonlinear, spiritual sense.) Don't think that daydreaming is a waste of time. Make use of it. Fall in love with your dreams, and push yourself to not only relax into them but to also develop them into conscious thoughts, and your organizing life will change.

Your dreams give you valuable insights into what your deepest desires are; they are here to help you to see what is possible. During the day (when you aren't imagining various scenes of worst-case outcomes), you dream a lot about experiencing something better in the future. Allow your dreams to fuel the fire of your actions. When you daydream, you fantasize about what things could be like, things that could be turned into a reality. Imagine yourself fulfilling your desire, and focus your attention on the details of that image in your mind. Allow time to bring with it a healing creativity and order. You can live a life of purposeful organizing solutions and inspired action.

When your thoughts and dreams are on organizing, perhaps you imagine your errands completed by noon of each day, or actually getting to the gym in the morning *and* to work on time. As you hold these visions in the forefront of your everyday experience and stay in this abundance of thoughts, your dreams will take on some kind of form. One manifestation might be that you arrive at class a few minutes before it starts. You now have the opportunity to get a good seat, open up your laptop, and be ready to focus on the teacher when the class starts. You reveal the self-control that you know lies within.

When you live in a state where your dreams come to life, you automatically perpetuate it. It is actually quite powerful to consciously dream deeply. Daydreaming about the future in a positive way, where you see it happening before your eyes, allows the experience to shortly follow. Ernest Holmes said, "The student should take time every day to see his life as he wishes it to be, to make a mental picture of his ideal." Being a conscious dreamer, and letting your dreams alter your conscious mind, shifts your experience. When you want to organize something in your life, for example your incoming mail, you have to see it first being accomplished if it is ever going to happen. You can take a moment, pause, and let your imagination set sail, seeing yourself bringing in the mail, sorting through it immediately, opening each item, filing those you need to keep, discarding those you don't, neatly setting those that need your later attention in their proper spaces. Think of how grateful your spouse or roommate will be!

You can do this with virtually any activity that you want to see run more smoothly and efficiently. In deciding to pick up this book, you told the universe that you're ready to organize something (or some things) in your life. What is your organizing goal? Even if it feels very intimidating, there is a power inside of you to make it possible. What does it feel like to be organized? Do you get a rush of adrenaline as you think about it?

Your daydreams are a manifestation of your creativity—send them into the universe and make them a manifestation of your reality! A spiritual time management program doesn't require you to better use your iCal app (of course, you can if you want to!). It requires you to pay attention to what you're imagining. If you can imagine it and believe it, you can have it.

And yes, there is a way to be in the creative mode and open to the possibility of space in your calendar. To go into the dream world, there are some basic meditation practices that can assist you. Note that the following steps don't follow a traditional meditation, in which you sink into a state of nonthinking: first, *concentration*— where you focus on a concept, word, breath, or something external, second, *mindfulness*—staying in the present moment with awareness, and third, *insightfulness*—drifting into dreamlike possibility.

You may have been told in grade school, "Stop daydreaming, and pay attention!" but I'd rephrase the advice: "Start daydreaming, and pay attention!" Think about your daydream, visualize how you would feel when it is true, and let the universe do its work. Krishnamurti once said, "Meditation is the ending of thought. It is only then that there is a different dimension that is beyond time." When my life gets busy, I personally enjoy counting my breaths: inhale one and exhale two. Count to ten and then repeat it. By slowing down, the timelessness of that present moment arises in my awareness, and if I want to, I can relax into the dream of my higher self.

* * *

Contemplation: Your Imagination

I quiet my mind and open my heart.
I breathe in and out several times.
All is quiet and all is well.

Pause for a moment, and let your imagination drift. What is your most common thought about getting organized? You live in a universe that is alive, creative, and ready to fulfill your dream. What is your organizing desire? The God of your own heart plants the dream in your imagination, so be cognizant and say your intention aloud, as your words when spoken aloud allow you to hear them and to be affected by them to act in that direction. This is your real power. No one is listening or watching, so raise the bar high, set your sights on a place where nothing and no one will get in your way. Plant your desire in the dream that is your imagination and see what happens.

Affirm: *I open up to thinking about what could be. I allow my imagination to be brought into full view, fully supported and encouraged, as it is a way that God speaks to me. I take time to see what is pulling me along and to either nurture it or let it go. I know that my active imagination, my thoughts and feelings, create my reality. I live as though I am there—living an organized life now.*

• • •

In this section, I explored how spiritual time management asks you to slow down your mind and to listen to your positive subconscious dreams along with your deliberate thoughts. In a spiritual time management system, you acknowledge the ineffable quality of time when you allow the Spirit to move you throughout your day. Your daily activities should not wipe you out but bring you happiness and joy, and honor the sacredness of your life. Punctuate your day with a God quality that can help you remain mindful of the presence of the Spirit in your life. Release, once and for all, the feeling that you aren't getting enough done. Befriend time; enjoy it! Open your heart to a new and peaceful existence where you are free to experience life in all its fullness.

PART IV

YOUR SPACE

*A high quality of life has a lot more to do with
what you remove from your life than what you add to it.*
—CHERYL RICHARDSON

Having worked in the organizing trenches for nearly two decades, and as the author of now three organizing books, I've noticed that a number of recent circumstances have given rise to what seems to be an unprecedented amount of disorganization. Advertising now bombards people everywhere they look (even at work—if you're on the internet, you're subjected to relentless ads), and the ability to shop anywhere, anytime now allows people perpetual opportunities to make purchases. When you look around your home or office, you can see just what is happening. The world in which you now live in is constantly telling you that it's better to have than to be. Taken to heart, these messages cost you your money, your time, and the quality of your life.

The advertising industry knows very well that in order to sell things to people, things that they really don't need, consumers must believe that those things will improved their lives. And because people are narcissistic, advertisers will often appeal to their self-image. They do this, for example, by telling you that a product will help you stand out from the crowd; that it will generate a life that is fun and/or that it will somehow make you more fully yourself. Tolle says we're not buying products, but identity enhancers. Designer labels (and even "anti-designer" labels, like Volvo) serve primarily as collective "identifiers" that people align themselves with. What keeps the consumer machine going is the fact that people's efforts to find themselves by collecting things doesn't work.

As you struggle along, it's no wonder that your space has fallen into disarray. When you finally wake up, you realize that you have so many things all over your house and your workplace that you no longer can remember what you even have. How many pens, socks, shoes, tools, towels, Tupperware containers (lid location unknown), do you have? Do you have any idea? Could you easily find the one you wanted? An array of mismanaged stuff is a typical result of practices that aren't working, and in fact, although you may not be consciously aware of it, this volume of stuff is generating stress in your life.

What you have around you in your various environments is important to your overall well-being and happiness. Today's lifestyle provides you with a lot of space to fill with a lot of stuff. And fill it we do! If you're like many people, you seem to have a natural tendency to accumulate things and to have a difficult time letting go of them. Why is that? Are you simply responding to advertising, always instilling you with the idea that this or that one thing will fulfill you? When you can't feel the life that you are, you're likely to try to fill up your life with things. Indeed, a large part of many people's lives is consumed by an obsessive preoccupation with things. I can't help but think about homes that were built before 1980—many had very small closets and very limited storage space. People then spent time with their neighbors rather than shopping at the mall, or scrolling through endless screens on Amazon.

I know deep down inside that order and peace in my surroundings will bring me greater peace of mind; the two work hand in hand. I'd rather open up my heart than my wallet and cultivate a deep relationship with people than with things. I also know that when I no longer care particularly about a possession (for any number of reasons), it feels like a drag on my body. It becomes a bother rather than a blessing. Even as a professional organizer, I let my things play games with my mind. It takes a good deal of physical energy and mental focus to keep my stuff in a reasonable order, but when I've let order fall by the wayside, I feel myself get out of sync.

One way to stay in sync with yourself and to move in the direction of your personal fulfillment is to seek out things that nurture you and further you in leading a life of mindfulness. I know that when I feel an urge to shop (and invariably start cluttering up my space), the best thing for me is to turn to nature. If I go on a hike, walk my dogs, or in another way just connect to my surroundings, that desire to fill up just goes away. Spend time on cultivating real skills and abilities to give you some grounding when the urge arises and you feel the need to consume.

Remember, your journey isn't about how much stuff you have but about your experiences and relationships and how they open your heart and connect you to the core truth of your being. When I purchase something, especially a toy for my children, I pause, take a deep breath, and ask myself, "Do we really need this? Will our lives be better if I buy it?" If I think that the answers are yes, I then ask, "How much time will it take to maintain this item?" (I've learned that my enthusiasm for picking up Lego pieces tends to fade pretty quickly.) I feel quite empowered by taking one minute to answer these questions; they help me clarify the wisdom of my purchasing choices.

Organizing things begins by exercising the power of choice before you get to the store or the yard sale or go online. Since mental clutter is at the root of your disorganization, the mind, of course, is where you begin. Clarity in your mind about what possessions mean for you and shifting that meaning, are key to creating clear spaces in your life. Don't forget that the universe responds to what you tell it; it doesn't make judgments about the truth of your message. It takes you at face value. So, when you can't release your items in a reasonable way or begin to hoard things, the universe believes that you have everything you need. If you keep things because you think you might need them someday and jam your home with possessions, you're telling the universe that you're "full," that you aren't open to receive. It is much wiser to let go of things that you no longer use and allow yourself to freely engage in the flow of circulation. Why not give up things that don't suit you and allow someone in need to benefit from your donations? The day-to-day choices that you make cause a spiritual ripple outward. Why spend your life accumulating material objects that will only turn to dust and ashes?

If you'd like to live more successfully and more conscientiously, you can release yourself from the unruly burden of overstuffed drawers and closets. There are people and organizations that need your stuff. I give a lot of my extra bedding, towels, and the like to the local animal shelter, "Best Friends," and it makes me feel happy to release those things to them. I feel like I'm making a difference. Also, in the long term, the time spent keeping your possessions in a state of order and readiness is much less than the time spent going through drawers looking for that screwdriver with the yellow handle, the socks that come up above your ankle, a black pen that actually writes. Isn't your time more valuable than that?

In *The High Price of Materialism*, author Tim Kasser states that what makes people happy are feelings of security, of their own competence, and of community. He goes on to say that when people hold materialistic values and organize their lives around attaining wealth and possessions, they are essentially wasting their time as far as their well-being is concerned. I think many of us know—but often lose site of the fact—that the qualities of self-assurance and inner stillness are not found at the mall. We lose our understanding of the preciousness of life when we chase and exalt things that are outside of ourselves. Peace can't be bought in a store.

The act of releasing clutter sets the stage for a consciousness of the new. It redefines perception and allows spaciousness so that the Spirit can do its work. In releasing distracting thoughts, you create space for a new thought, a better thought, a divine idea. You are honoring your good but not limiting your greatness. Similarly, by releasing possessions that don't have much value to you, you make room for something that does.

You may have noticed that we human adults are rather preoccupied with the physical aspects of our lives. Many people are caught in the trap of buying what they don't really need and then holding on to it long past its prime. This habit is not easy to break, as it's part of the cycle of working at an unsatisfying job in order to pay for the things that were just purchased. Some of those things are considered so precious that the people feel they must insure them and thus have another reason to work at the not-so-great job. Sadly, many people wind up burying their true nature and the happiness that comes with it under piles of acquisitions (and credit card bills!).

The piles of acquisitions invariably reflect the expectation that they will bring about self-enhancement. If you try to find yourself through them, you lose. The only perceived path to progress is always just more things; it is never over. Most material consumption is driven by desire or fear. Desire is the wish to have something so that you can be yourself more fully. Fear is usually driven by the possibility of losing something and thereby becoming diminished and being less-than. And so, clutter is a manifestation of fear. Look your clutter straight in the eye, and let it know that you're the boss. It is remarkably empowering! Science has shown that highly materialistic people are less happy than those less attached to things. This is the first step on your path to freedom.

And get this! Being happy is not only its own reward but when you feel happy you're also temporarily smarter, friendlier, and more productive. The feeling of growth and movement toward an organizing goal is very important to happiness; it's just as important as reaching the goal. Yes, the journey is the destination. Create your path in advance by thinking of the way you want it to go, and you will create an organized life.

CHAPTER TEN
VISUAL PEACE

Simplicity, whether chosen or forced upon us, is still a gift.
—JACK KORNFIELD

At the time that I was growing up in the 1970s, the middle class was ascending in its economic power, and people were experiencing rising wages, raising smaller families and enjoying more money for discretionary expenditures. During that time, people began spending a smaller percentage of their household budget on necessities, like utilities and food, and found that they had both more money and more time in which to spend it. (It does not seem to be a coincidence that The National Association of Professional Organizers was started in the early 1980s.)

My parents were both very mindful about how they spent their hard-earned money. We had nice things but not an overabundance of things. My mom took great pride in what she had, and we always felt like we had enough of everything. I was blessed that my family was able to provide my basic needs. But even with the reasonableness of my parents' treatment of money and things, I was educated by the world in which I live, and I've often thought if I just had more stuff, more belongings around me, that my life would be better and that I would feel better about myself. As I became older, I made more money and moved around a lot. I bought and purged and bought and purged again, until it finally hit me that getting more stuff was not connected to more joy or a better life. I came to realize how much space and energy all my belongings required. It takes up a lot of your valuable time to maintain what you already own.

The Buddha believed that the root of suffering is to be found in constant wanting and craving. People pay for their covetousness in some way or form. For me, and I believe for most people, the outer space that my belongings take up costs me more than just time and money. Studies have shown that visual clutter reduces your brain's ability to process information. The amount of visual distractions that you have at home or at work rob you from finding a sense of balance and peace in the moment. For me, empty space is freedom, freedom to connect to nature and beyond. The less I need, the less energy it takes to take care of what I have. I urge you to seek out low-maintenance things and fewer of them; fewer tins of tea or winter socks or pairs of jeans. Stuff is energy and if your eyes are at ease, so too will be your mind.

• • •

THE STRESS OF STUFF

No one outside of ourselves can rule us inwardly.
—JACK KORNFIELD

The high level of stress that many people experience may lead them straight to the doctor or even the hospital. So many health issues are stress-related as we are clearly living in a very anxiety-producing, anxiety-filled world. The fastest way to fix the problems in your life is to remove your stressors. (It's also probably the hardest!) The stress that arises in you when you can't find your subway card or your car keys can be greatly diminished if you value a different way of being. Many clients have said, "I just can't believe how much energy I was putting into finding things."

One of the big stressors of life today stems from people's need for approval. If you're like most people, you feel that in order to be accepted and liked, you must wear certain clothes and maintain a certain type of appearance. This is a costly activity and because you must always refresh your look (keeping up with styles, getting your hair cut, whitening your teeth again), it is nearly impossible to get off the wheel of always needing new stuff to be happy and admired. The quickest way to feel good is to consume something and think about your suffering later. You can't help but feel that some *thing* is going to make you happy (or at least happier than you are). If you like to keep up with the Joneses—if you look for your self-worth from outside sources and need a lot of external validation, you will value possessions that you believe have more panache than others.

Your mind is constantly being filled up by clutter, both material things and things to think about and do. Thoughts just keep pouring out of you, and most of your thoughts are not even relevant to what you're experiencing—most of them are about the past or the future. No wonder you feel so out of balance. Remember that you are not in fact a slave to your stuff: if you're a slave, it's to your thoughts, which drive you to replenish the stuff, "patching" the external in lieu of healing the internal.

Rather than object consciousness, which Eckhart Tolle describes as our "sense perceptions, thoughts, emotions, and whatever happens in our lives," you should seek space consciousness, in which you begin to see the illusion of the material world and experience less of it controlling your life. Releasing clutter prepares the consciousness for new experiences to flow. It enhances perception of the next step to take, as well as gives the Spirit room to do its work. Releasing anything, thoughts that hold you back or bags of stuff that you will never ever use, will alleviate your stress and you will be able to better create a place of refuge.

It is stressful to always be in a state of anticipation—always wanting more, better, faster, whatever it is that isn't happening right here and right now. This wanting, Tolle says, "keeps the ego alive much more than having." He goes on to say that nothing will ever satisfy it, no matter how much you do or don't have. As it buries itself into you, like a New England tick, it calls forth your negative, glass-half-empty self, and you complain about what you don't have, what you desperately need, and how you would do anything to have it. The ego is always crying out for attention and is always ready to take down the person it occupies, if it isn't satisfied. Watch out. Put out the fire by being and not doing. When you are outside of the present and become distracted by your thoughts and your environment, you lose.

The deep emotion, that the need for ever more stuff comes from is a fear—fear of not being noticed, of not feeling special or successful. As I said earlier, clutter is a manifestation of fear, a fear of being the imperfect self that you think you are. Only the revelation of your true self, what you're made of and what is possible, will set you free of the ego. When you experience your true, connected self, you no longer feel the need to compare yourself with others and to see yourself through others' eyes. As Tolle says, "The ego tends to equate having with Being: I have, therefore, I am. And the more I have, the more I am."

Once you've developed your inner self, so you don't unnecessarily buy things, you can work on loosening your emotional attachment to the things you have. Remember that every addiction, shopping included, comes into focus when you can no longer run from its pain. (You have too much stuff to deal with, and it is killing you!) But if you turn toward that ego and challenge it, it soon collapses. The entire advertising industry would no longer be around if you stopped relying on material items to provide you with your identity. The more you seek fulfillment in the world outside of you, the less satisfied you will be with your life.

There are over 40,000 items in a typical American grocery store, thousands of items in the average home. With this kind of abundance (if that's what you want to call it), you really need to know yourself in order to not get hooked into the wants and desires that truly aren't even your own. Getting off this wheel and into your own groove is the real stress buster. Doing what works for you and moves you forward, and feeling empowered to do what is the best possible thing you can do for yourself, are much more rewarding than a new handbag will ever be. Much of one's day is filled with working and spending, and the simple pleasures of life are too often ignored. Embracing simplicity is partly about the number of material things we own, but more importantly, it's about maintaining the pleasures that renew you as part of the web of life. This week, think about the pleasures that you most enjoy as the days go by. Walk around your house and take stock.

Chaos exacts a significant energetic toll. When the space you occupy is filled with random old items, it is like living in a polluted swamp. Energy is blocked from entering; stagnation sets in. The state of your drawers is a clear reflection of the state of your subconscious mind. The space outside of you is a reflection of your inner space. As Joan Borysenko says, "If you want more inner peace, take the time to establish outer peace." Be critical of (yet gentle toward) what you are surrounding yourself with. And be aware that during the organizing process, a sense of exhaustion and confusion may enter your space. Since organizing makes demands on your belief systems—such as the belief, for example, that you have to keep that horrible purple vase because your aunt gave it to you—I strongly encourage you to get some support and help in the thick of it. You may need to hire a professional organizer (www.napo.net), or a good friend who isn't critical would be ideal. Take it seriously, honor the process, and find a place to feel rejuvenated and at peace. You can create that environment—now!

* * *

Contemplation: The Need for a Refuge

I quiet my mind and open my heart.
I breathe in and out several times.
All is quiet and all is well.

Creating a refuge is important when you feel overwhelmed by all the activities that you have to do day in and day out. Because stressors are all around you and you always have the potential to become overwhelmed, you want to have a place in which you can comfortably just relax into the experience of your higher self. Of course, your goal is to have your entire home reflect the feeling of peace you have inside. In the meantime, carve out a corner of your favorite room and tidy it up. Fight off stress by using that sacred place as your refuge as you move along your organizing journey.

Affirm: *I seek out a place of safety and stillness when I feel overwhelmed by trying to get organized. I find a place to examine what is* *happening, and when I feel overwhelmed and exhausted, I stop and allow myself to realign. The stress in my life that I encounter is now gone. The Spirit lives within me and expresses itself through me. I am now revitalized and energized by what lies ahead. I have a sacred space, a refuge in fighting off my stress.*

. . .

JOYFUL PURGING

What ought one to say, then, as each hardship comes?
I was practicing for this. I was training for this.
—EPICTETUS

Many of us use shopping as a mental distraction; in reality, shopping is a forum for running from something while believing that something else right around the corner is going to make us happier. Ask yourself, "What do I truly enjoy about shopping? Does it help to fulfill my real needs, or only my short-term emotional needs? When I bring something new home, how much do I enjoy it? How much am I enjoying it a week after I've bought it? How much am I enjoying it a year later?"

Professional Organizer, Julie Morgenstern, says that clutter is "any object, space, commitment, or behavior that distracts you or weighs you down, thus depleting your energy and your ability to focus and get things done." And since you live in a culture of consumption where instant gratification is the norm, you do a lot of emotional buying. When you become emotionally charged, you become rationally challenged. If you're feeling lonely or sad or anxious, for example, that limits the capacity of your prefrontal cortex to regulate your behavior and makes you more vulnerable to mindless TV viewing, where advertisers are ready to pounce.

151

Where you get into trouble is with the obsessive, endless shopping you likely engage in. It has an immediate impact on your feelings: shopping has been shown to elevate one's dopamine levels, and it literally makes you feel good, at least in the short run. And for some people, it is truly addictive. According to the American Journal of Psychiatry, 5.8 percent of the population are compulsive shoppers. The "law of accumulation" is the exact opposite of the law that sustains and promotes a meaningful life—business executives know this, and design a world in which we focus on having rather than being.

There are some basic questions that I always ask myself before I buy another gym outfit (both in the market and online): a) Do I really need another set of black leggings? Pause, wait for the answer. b) How will I pay for it? Remember that the longer you remain in a store or online, the more you spend, so make a point of getting what you need and quickly departing. It is not a coincidence that as you scroll through your Facebook posts, you see the item that you were just looking at on a website. Everyone around you wants you to buy things, spend money and do it all again! Invasive is the word I use when describing how closely our internet activity is being monitored (and used to seduce us!).

You might find that you're particularly susceptible to buying something because it is on sale or because you just want to have something new; you don't realize the effort it will take to maintain it and even pay for it. Another roasting pan in your kitchen, another *tchotchke* on your office desk; each is also another thing you will have to deal with in the future. It may seem inconsequential, but in no time, you wind up with thousands of items spread throughout your home and workspace. I've worked with many families that have been responsible for putting their deceased parents' stuff in order, and the time and energy such a project takes (not to mention the frequent family feuds that it generates) is debilitating.

Or course, another issue is simply the money you compulsively spend and what that does to the rest of your life. Do your shopping habits align with your budget? Do you have credit card bills that you can't pay off at the end of month? I recommend a budget like this: 50 percent of your take-home pay to must-haves (like housing or food); 30 percent to wants; 20 percent to savings. Never work to sustain a lifestyle, and always think more about saving than spending. Say to yourself, "Today I simplify my life and step into a state of clarity and peace."

And when you do shop, remember that you live in a global market place; every dollar you spend or don't spend is the equivalent of a vote for a certain future. Be mindful of patronizing businesses that don't respect human rights, animal rights, and planetary rights. Give thanks for the money you hold in your hand for the abundance of goods to choose from, for the discernment to make wise purchases for the future of our planet. Think of the environment before you shop.

When you release your belongings, books, clothes or useless kitchen items, you have to trust in the process that a greater good is unfolding. Your drive to accumulate is so strong that purging becomes a very challenging thing. So much is brought to the surface and then not knowing what to do with it all can make your head spin. Holmes stated, "Today is the time in which we should cut loose from the threads of previous experiences, whenever they were negative, and deliberately make up our minds that we shall no longer create our future out of the old past."

Your act of purging, of letting go, will change your life and the world around you. You will possess fewer things, waste less money, worry less, and pollute the planet less. It is your job to lighten your load, whether with stuff or just thoughts that don't serve you—you are the one that has to clear your own path. How fortunate that you're also the one who can bring about change in your life. If you can remember the four principles that everything is alive, interconnected, conscious, and always changing, then you go with the movement of life and not against it.

Your number one job is to heal your thought patterns and to be reminded that the creative medium is impersonal and gives you what you think you need to be happy. You give it form and make it personal by what you are thinking about. For example, when you say, "I don't have enough yet," what you're really saying to yourself is, "I am not enough," or "I need more of," and you dwell on that. Conditions are created by your thoughts, and your belief creates your life. External reality always reflects back to you your inner state. Let go of the past, lay down the burdens, and move toward the greater good within you. When you let go of things that no longer serve you, you will then create a space that will support you now.

Change takes time. (Oh, say it isn't so!) Organizing takes time. Sorting and purging take time. Once you develop a rhythm, it's actually fun and begins to take on a life of its own. It will help energize you further, staying on plan and feeling in control. How do you let go of your attachment to things? It is a challenge, as people are natural nesters, and as I said earlier, today's society exalts consumerism. The desire for material items goes away when you no longer find your identity in them. I always thought that a good name for an organizing book would be *Space = Peace*. We make 35,000 decisions a day; make smart ones about organizing—embrace organizing routines, and set some long-term goals. I would suggest developing a mantra; "The peace of God guides me in bringing harmony to my relationships with my things."

When you become organizationally aware of your surroundings and develop a spatial awareness for the space you live in, you will be stronger in letting go, and you will be able to get away from the controlling ego. Detach yourself from consumption, and then inner peace will emerge. The ego will always be challenging you to get more and have more. It will never be satisfied and will want your smaller self to grasp at things. But there is no such thing as an addiction to an object. There is only addiction to the experience of purchasing it and the burst of energy that it gives us in that moment. When you start to purge, you will undoubtedly feel that the "rush" of peace that is made available by your now easily accessible closet is much more gratifying.

Evaluating your stuff starts from an intention, and as then you open to that intention, it becomes firmly anchored internally. Once you raise your consciousness and your connection to the Spirit, you will desire less, and reveal more, of what you want to happen. When I'm setting out to clean up a particular space, I say to myself, "If I can deal with the mental clutter, I will be able to deal with the physical clutter." And as I release from my mind, I move toward a greater experience of what will be. Remember that clearing your mind opens the space for your creativity to be activated. Ask yourself, "What needs to be released in order to clear and be available for my good?" Set a goal and complete that area before you begin another. It is time for the outside to match the inside. And so I say to myself, "Today I activate a willingness to hear guidance in showing me the way to organization and peace."

Don't be surprised to find that your resistance to the task at hand stalks you. You may find yourself thinking, "I don't have time to do this now," or "This task is so overwhelming, I'll never manage it." Your smaller self is trying to keep you hooked. Be bold, be willing and ready to embrace a new life.

a) Start with a vision. Start small.

b) Pick one thing to work on for thirty days. (Dealing with mail or the foyer in your home.)

c) Continue to visualize how you feel when this task is complete.

d) Reward yourself when you complete an area.

Harness the power of routine to accomplish some long-procrastinated tasks. Finish one organizing area and it will generate positive energy and motivation to continue. Remember that you are at the center of time, and as little successes turn into big successes, the accompanying little boosts of happiness make you smarter and more connected to your center.

Happiness isn't located in something outside of you but is found when you're fully complete and present and honest in the moment. If you suffer from a consciousness of "lack," it is your job to focus on abundance instead. By clinging to an idea that is contrary to abundance, you further separate yourself from a peaceful relationship with time and space. If you can put your mind into an arena in which you can receive, you are well on your way. Purging yourself of the items that you don't need is an extension of that mind-set; it's a way of telling the universe that you're ready for exciting new things in your life.

Constantly tell yourself that you have everything you need, and when you begin to feel deeply fulfilled, the desires of stuff and gathering no longer fill up your life—and your space. Your home exists as a place for you to rest, to find refuge in a busy world that always wants your attention. Your workplace exists as a place for you to use your talents and your skills, to create something or provide a service. Rather than just try to fill those spaces up, find a connection and affinity with your spaces, and be aware of them, nurture those relationships. Create spaces in your life where your inner needs are fed and your higher ideals become more apparent. Release, rather than acquire, in your actions, and you will be better able to see your purpose and allow your abilities to shine.

* * *

Contemplation: When Stuck, Move

I quiet my mind and open my heart.
I breathe in and out several times.
All is quiet and all is well.

It is so easy for us to get in a funk and stay in it, thinking that there is nothing more oppressive than getting oneself organized. It is easy to think you don't have the right container or that it isn't going to last. Negativity breeds negativity, so stay in circulation, and when you feel trapped and not able to move forward, reassess and move into a place where you feel safe and can take a breather. I appreciate the saying, "Move a muscle, change a thought." Once up and running again, go in the direction of your happiness and your joy.

Affirm: *I let go and let God in. I'm an instrument of harmony. When feeling overwhelmed, I move my thoughts into a space of positivity, thinking and then doing anything that uplifts my spirit. I am powerful enough to move through anything and land in a place where I'm better supported and nurtured. I let go of the past, release what no longer serves my highest self and open the way for greater good, always being thankful for what I currently have. I'm blessed. And so it is.*

CHAPTER ELEVEN
LIVING SPACE

There's no place like home.
—THE WIZARD OF OZ

The state of your living space is critical to the quality of your daily experience. Organizing is about making life as easy as possible—creating easy systems to find what you need, when you need it. When you feel rested and calm, you can connect your mind to your higher self, where your deeper needs are nurtured and you're inspired to act. As your spiritual life becomes a greater focus for you, the desire for more material possessions lessens. The reverse is also true.

My goal is to make your house into a sanctuary where you are rejuvenated; a place from which you can move in the right direction and cultivate qualities that lead to an overall healthier life. Remember that your home reflects your state of mind, and if you want to be happy, to be free to lead by your heart, your home must not be in disarray. My mom used to say, "A clear desk is a clear mind," and I would add, "a clear mind has vision and perspective." Be still and hear the voice inside, leading you in the right direction.

A home stuffed with possessions derails your equanimity. As Karen Kingston, the author of *Clear Your Clutter with Feng Shui*, states, "Feng Shui is the art of balancing and harmonizing the flow of natural energies in our surroundings to create beneficial effects in our lives." Unlike at work, where you might not feel free to express your most authentic self, your home offers you a place to be just that. If you look around your personal space, does it reflect a peaceful, organized mind? If not, your home, your purported "sanctuary," is just another cause of stress and anxiety. Such stress increases the tension you feel in your body. It elevates the rawness of your emotions and sucks at your intellect, making it all the more challenging to "bring it down" and relax. Does the state of your home reflect a jumbled state of mind?

When people speak of clutter, very specific images often come to mind. "When I went to visit a college friend and walked into her living room, there was so much stuff everywhere I couldn't breathe." "The house is so full you feel like you're drowning." "The paperwork and mess in my office is suffocating me. It stinks." Of course, these are just examples, but note that they share the feeling of gasping for air. I know that when I'm in a messy space, I often feel buried alive. This is a psychological state as well as a physical one (the dust, dust mites, and stuffy air play a part in the sense of breathlessness).

Clearing up the clutter is good for your body, your mind, and your soul. Think of how much easier it is to access a deep space of peace when not surrounded by an environment of chaos and clutter. In fact, it is deeply empowering to remove the excess stuff from your life. It means that you've let go of the fear of what lurks in your quiet mind. Do you, if you're honest with yourself, seek to distract yourself from a truly quiet state of mind? It's likely you label a feeling of intellectual discomfort as boredom, but is it? Are you bored, or do you feel just a bit of anxiety start to arise when you aren't occupied by some kind of chore, worry, or entertainment? What do you do when your brain doesn't need to be actively engaged in a particular endeavor or exercise? Do you pick up a magazine, turn on the TV, make a phone call, surf the internet? Do you mask the mental sense of lack and discomfort with a bodily desire and satisfy it briefly by eating, drinking, or smoking? Do you get in the car and go to the mall? (This is a particularly effective distraction because it provides a space that is not your messy, stress-inducing home.)

The thought of a decluttered home can actually be frightening! Learning to trust and let go isn't something that comes naturally to you. You needn't run from your overstuffed home. Decide to embrace a new space in which you keep only the things that you need or that actually bring you joy. Your home is in balance because you are. While you think that you yearn for the chance to spend quiet time in the silence of your own soul, you always feel like you need to do something else right now. The clutter you surround yourself with is both a physical and a psychological impediment to your experience of your most spacious self. Change comes with choice, and each decision you make to disconnect from unneeded stuff moves you closer to a less anxious, healthier life.

Like most people, you're probably resistant to change. I believe that it is not the change itself that bothers people; it's the thought of losing something. This is such a deeper conversation than the 322 ways to get organized! Purging is tough—letting go and not knowing what is around the corner isn't an easy thing to do. People can't help but have a tremendous aversion to loss; social analysts find that humans tend to overvalue things that they have. We connect deeply to our stuff.

We tend to work harder to avoid losses (or avoid pain) than to achieve gains (or achieve pleasure). An example of this is the finding that golfers will try harder to avoid a bogey (the loss of points for going over par) than to achieve a birdie (the gain of points for being under par). The aversion to loss will compel people to do things that are simply illogical. Your living space matters—stop consuming so much, learn to let go, and trust that divine order is waiting to be expressed in your life.

• • •

ATTACHMENT

We consume to forget our worries and our anxieties.
Tranquilizing ourselves with over-consumption is not the way.
—THICH NHAT HANH

Somewhere in your soul, you know that your attachment to things is robbing you of something important in your life. I've mentioned previously that one of the most basic levels of self-identification is through either owning or associating with things. When you're overly devoted to owning things, you mistake an external object for the internal state of peace. In fact, when you identify with something, you endow it with a sense of your very self; it becomes, in an abstract way, part of who you are.

The truth about the role that your stuff plays in your life can be found in your gut response to thoughts about your personal assets. You tell yourself that you "need" them, but do they provide you with delight? Are you listening to old, unexamined ideas in your mind and acting out old, unexamined behavior patterns in response?

The idea of scarcity, no matter how unrealistic, tugs at many people, and hoarding becomes the habit. As I mentioned earlier, people have a great aversion to losing the things they have. Sadly, the belief in limitation causes you to not only create an anxiety-producing environment, it encourages the accumulation of excessive credit card debt, further cluttering your mind with anxiety, fear, and guilt. You then question yourself, and regret, worry, and shame intrude upon the spiritual space where joy, contentment, and creativity could otherwise reside.

Any kind of clutter, from random papers to one-too-many end tables, creates an obstacle to the smooth flow of energy in a space. This in turn creates inertia and confusion in the lives of the occupants. Clutter destroys positive energy. So, the clutter begins as a symptom of what is happening within your life and then compounds the problem by attracting more stagnant energy.

Whenever I come across clutter, its energy field is unmistakable. It has an unpleasant, sticky, and dirty feeling. And I know that if there is clutter in a space, it is first created in the invisible clutter that is in the occupant's mind. Perhaps you suffer from "poverty consciousness," and you keep things around because you don't trust that they will be there in the future. Your things serve as reminders of who you think you are and give you a sense of security. If you have a lot of clutter around, it is frequently a demonstration of your attachment to the past. Clutter is anything that no longer serves you, and if you think of your possessions as representing your past, they can keep you living in the past.

Clutter is about self-protection. You may feel seduced by the "safety" your stuff purportedly provides, but in truth, it gives you little clarity about your true purpose. Clutter makes you feel depressed and unmotivated by it. The accumulation of too much stuff is invariably tied to an accumulation of self-defeating thoughts, beliefs, and feelings you've been repeating to yourself. When I enter a home with a clutter problem, there are a slew of other problems that lurk behind the scenes.

Clutter holds you back, depresses you, weighs you down, and blocks new experiences from flowing into your life. It also creates more work for you as the more stuff you have, the more you have to clean and manage and the more distracted you are by your environment. The less cluttered your surroundings are, the simpler your life becomes. Imagine what the clutter in your head is doing to you—this alone is reason to get rid of the clutter outside of your head!

Simplifying your life will go far in returning you to balance. Yes, letting go of your stuff feels difficult before you start, but once you do, you will realize how freeing it is. It's like losing a bunch of excess weight overnight. Indeed, organizing your possessions brings you greater clarity about the purpose of your life. When you consider the stacks of DVDs piled up in the living room, you might ask yourself, "Do they lift my energy when I think about them and look at them? Or do these items just obscure my vision?" If the answer is the latter, the stacks of DVDs just represent one more speed bump on your path to peace of mind. Another thing to consider is how the excess stuff in your home plays havoc with your time. How much time have you wasted over the past year looking in the junk drawer for a pen that actually works? How many times have you spent searching on your computer for that cucumber salad recipe you liked so much? Being disorganized drags you down. By letting go of the things that you don't need or use and organizing those that you do, freedom is at your beck and call.

Spiritual teachers from many religious paths advise living in the present. Decluttering isn't just simplifying your life; it's about having a vision and setting new priorities to make that vision a reality. How do you picture the life that you want? Your home reflects your state of mind. Holding on to items from long ago (the dress you wore to the junior prom, your dad's train set, your grandparents' "everyday" china, all the birthday cards you've ever received), doesn't make your past any different from what it was. Items from long ago don't bring people back from the dead. They're rarely of much monetary value and will not increase in value with time. "Memory" clutter can take up so much room in your home that it compromises your quality of life.

You can't control the future. You often think that you "might need it someday," and so you hang on to all sorts of things that don't serve you. Don't procrastinate any longer. Every time you decide to remove something that no longer serves you or you refrain from impulsively buying something you don't really need or have the space for, you are blessing yourself. Your material items should inspire you to create the next steps. In my experience, removing the clutter permits someone to become the person he or she is inside; they replace possessions with freedom and hope. Your life right now is the priority. Open it up to something new by eliminating the stuff you don't use and creating some new space. Focus on your attachments to people and causes that are worthy of your time.

* * *

Contemplation: Let Go

I quiet my mind and open my heart.
I breathe in and out several times.
All is quiet and all is well.

Today is a good day to let go of all that no longer serves you in living a life of grace, joy, and beauty. You are perfect, whole, and complete right now. You lack for nothing, and you use the experiences of your life to direct your inner mind to know a greater truth. You constantly expand your willingness to know, to be, and to have your good.

Affirm: *All my needs are taken care of as I follow my higher power. I let go and let God take the wheel. I let go of everything that is no longer aligned with my highest good. I let go of all the negative thoughts that keep me trapped and unable to get organized. I free myself from the burden of stuff, and I am open to the creative energy of the universe. Today, I let God's love lead the way. I have a blessed life.*

• • •

DIVINE ORDER

Everything is possible to him who believes.
—MARK 9:23

Living in a decluttered home is not about "living with less" as much as it is about living with purpose and balance. I've never seen an organizing problem that wasn't a thinking problem. If you attach to the problem and do not choose order, you get more of the same old thing. When you choose a simple life, you choose to resist the pressures of materialistic consumerism. You choose to take control of your life, deciding how you live and what you buy. And your decisions are based on your values, not on an impulse or an advertiser's admonition. Getting organized is a way to make life easier. Once you purge yourself of the excess, what you're left with is clarity. You can see your purpose clearly, and your entire awareness shifts to a new, lighter level.

Spiritual organizing honors the sanctity of this experience, in creating a lifestyle that supports your higher self. It's the feel of the space, not just its appearance. Some homes have a positive, inviting ambiance, and happy people invariably occupy them. Even before I became a Professional Organizer, I always felt the connection between the inner and the outer environment. I wanted everything in order because it made me feel calmer.

Being in an orderly mental and physical environment frees the soul to seek the highest level of creativity possible. There is a deep sense of peace and belonging, a connection to life that happens when you treat your home as your sanctuary. By freeing your space, you free yourself. Your home contains an energy level and is a physical expression of the peace and calm you hope to experience within. You want your environment working for you, not against you. Trust that divine order is seeking you.

One of the most sacred tasks of your life is creating a home. Once you've created a well-organized, restful place in which you can find the things you want, it is imperative that you maintain it. You can set up lovely organizing systems, but unless you shift how you move through your world, the systems will be only minimally helpful. The shift comes in your beliefs. So, daily organizing is an element of a spiritual practice. Keeping an organized, uncluttered home speaks to your faith. We must be so grateful for what we have. Gratitude ignites the way for simplicity, where you desire less and be more.

When you recognize that all your physical (and emotional!) clutter begins first as a thought that you've latched onto, you can begin to dismantle it simply by reframing the thought the moment it arises. You can begin this very moment by looking subjectively at the thoughts you have about your possessions and then by asking yourself if these thoughts are true. What if you stopped believing the messages you give yourself over and over about the value of the stuff that's bursting out of your cabinets, dressers, and closets (and maybe is even all over the floor)? Such masses of clutter have powerful magnetic fields that attract similar things. How quickly things can deteriorate when you haven't dealt with the very basics of life.

So, if you want to change your circumstances, seek divine order in your life. Part of your job is to become aware of your current mental wiring; then rewire the way you put things together, so you can have a new, more desirable experience. Positive feelings accelerate the rewiring process, so it is worth the effort to encourage feelings of success and happiness. When you create a compelling vision—a strong mental picture—of your new order, your uncluttered spaces, what you want them to look like and feel like, and how you want to feel in them, you are doing even more to strengthen those new neural pathways and connections.

If you desire greater order and peace of mind, you can say to yourself, "I am so grateful for this holy order that is my life." Once again, the law of attraction is at work—as you focus on order and peace, more of both will come your way. Everything I've discussed about identifying and clearing your mental clutter will help you sort through and clear your physical clutter.

If you believe the universe responds to you, and that it is everywhere, in everything, then the universe must also be in the clutter. If the divine is everywhere, then the divine is in the clutter. If God is everywhere, then God is in the clutter. Thus, the clutter is something that the universe has brought to you because you have envisioned it in your mind, deliberately or not. The universe listens to what you say, so you can "un-envision" it. You can effectively replace the vision with a tidy, welcoming, peaceful space. Choose an attitude of gratitude for your new order, and your new order will manifest.

You are the master of your inner world, and you can create a space for peace inside yourself. There you can sink ever further into the presence of God, knowing that divine order prevails. By claiming that organizing is about making your life easier, it is easier to stay organized. If my house is "messy," I start in one place, the foyer. I begin with one thought that says, "I can get my foyer organized," and with each new challenge, I reaffirm divine order in my life.

* * *

Contemplation: Trust

I quiet my mind and open my heart.
I breathe in and out several times.
All is quiet and all is well.

When an obstacle appears, you can choose your response. You can choose a path of faith instead of fear and an attitude of abundance instead of scarcity. Give thanks for the divine order that is within you and around you. Affirm this divine order in yourself and expect good results to come forth. Rest in God, and surrender to the restorative power of silence.

Affirm: *The order and sacredness of the universe is expressed in every space in my home. Every room is in order, every space is in order, and harmony fills my life. Everything that is no longer of use or value to me is now discarded or circulated to where it is useful to others. My house is in order. My affairs are in order. I let go of thoughts that limit me, that no longer serve my growth. I am free of clutter, and it feels good! I trust God and move in the direction of my highest and best all the time. I trust that divine order is all around me.*

CHAPTER TWELVE
WORKING SPACE

Energy and persistence conquer all things.
—BENJAMIN FRANKLIN

So far you've learned that the consciousness you have creates your world. Thus, it creates the environment where you work, and the way you go about your professional life. The layout and energy that you bring to your office is critical to whether you create a forward-thinking space. It is like leaving an energetic scent—possessions infuse your environment and those around you with a certain feeling. If you find that it is hard to think clearly in your workplace or that it's hard to find something that you need to complete a project or assignment, you won't be flourishing in that space. Your performance, productivity, and your self-esteem will suffer.

Since I've been self-employed much of my professional life, I can work the way I want and when I want, but that requires much self-discipline and focus to succeed. I have found that a conscious, organized working system, at home or at work, gives me more control, more power, and even more motivation. It helps just knowing where things are and what is coming up on the schedule. I find that when I go through my vertical filing stand and purge papers, I feel lighter and better able to see what is coming up and what needs to get done. This control brings forth confidence that will be a great asset in all of your future endeavors. If you consciously create spaces that engender feelings of appreciation and worthiness, those who report to you will trust you and follow you. On the other hand, those who supervise you will appreciate your positive management style. In order to create such spaces, you must enter them every day with a mind that is free of anger and frustration.

When you start to let go of things that don't add value to your life, your life lightens up—you have literally less to think about and less to maintain. It is freeing to open up space around you; you'll find that your attitude lightens. Why not check some items off your list of things that weigh you down. When I purge two bankers' boxes of paper, or weed through a file cabinet drawer, it is so refreshing and freeing. You deserve a workspace that invites you to be productive and creative and that fosters the positive energy that you want to have as you come through the door. You devote a lot of your time and energy to what you do for a living, why not do what you can to spend that time inspired and happy?

Lastly, whether you work from home or at a hospital or a government office, you are the one in control of your space and how it functions. You control the energy you have at your place of work. If your work environment is not one in which personal items or spatial arrangements are overtly accommodated, try your best to create a personal space that, nonetheless, resonates with you. (That includes a good chair—yes, ergonomics matter!). You must do your best under such circumstances to create a workspace that calms you and speaks to who you are.

· · ·

SELF-HONORING

Give your dreams all you've got and you'll be amazed
at the energy that comes out of you.
—WILLIAM JAMES

To feel calm and capable at work requires organization and a desire to keep your space tidy and supportive, with what you need nearby. Considering the amount of stuff most people keep in their drawers and on their desks, it's not unlikely that you're constantly shuffling things around in an effort to locate something you need. I was recently organizing an office in a hospital, and it took me four hours to sort through medical journals and miscellaneous documents. In the end, most of these materials were thrown away. The energy was lifted in the room, and it felt that real purpose and dedication were alive and well.

When faced at work with an unwieldy amount of papers, ask yourself, "Are these documents of any true value to me in the future? How often do I actually refer back to these papers?" If you're holding onto things on the outside chance that you'll need them someday but find that you never really do, reconsider allowing them to collect dust on your desk. Your personal workspace matters; it affects your state of mind and thus how well you manage the tasks required of you during the day. Make it streamlined, having what you need at your fingertips and ready to take the next steps.

Just like in your home, your work environment is a physical manifestation of how you feel. I can typically walk into an office, and see the energy of the person, depressed or inspired, by how his or her workspace is set up. As things are arranged right now at your workspace, do they reinforce a cluttered, or peaceful, mind? We know that a clear space supports our mental clarity, our physical health, and our feelings of ease. Your soul needs an orderly environment in which to thrive. Why not step up, believe in yourself, and create a space that supports your intuition, your creativity, and the gifts you bring to your workplace? This is worth doing no matter what type of work life you're experiencing at the moment. The time you spend at work may be devoted to someone else's project or product, or well-being, but the time is still yours to experience. Why not make it as pleasant and fruitful as possible?

Rather than toss paper onto the "look at later" pile, I urge you to look at it once and decide to immediately toss it, file it, or act upon it. I know I'm not the only one to long for a clearer, simpler life by way of a less cluttered desk and a tidy desktop on my computer. But the solution to the problem of chaos is not always a head-on organizational attack. Getting organized is more than just affixing labels to files—the greatest value from an organized workspace is the ability to focus on your goals. Visual clutter isn't inspirational for many people. Taking a little time to set up shop and go through your paperwork at the end of each week (or month if that is more reasonable for you) would be ideal. Starting with a few extra minutes at the end of each workday, purge unnecessary papers and prepare for the next day.

A clear space fosters a clear mind. (And yes, a clear mind helps create a clear space!). If you have less stuff it means that you have more time, as you don't have to clean and organize so often. With less stuff, your workspace looks more spacious and calm. A compelling vision of your new order, what you want your workspace to look like and feel like, and how you want to feel in it, generates neural pathways that actually help make the vision a reality. I once heard during a Sunday sermon, "Pain pushes us until the vision pulls us." The discomfort of the chaos in your life is undoubtedly what pushed you to pick up this book. Let your vision of a tidy, attractive workspace pull you into its manifestation.

Organizing isn't something that many people look forward to. You may struggle to stay on the path, but if you find that you're frustrated, take advantage of the power of a mantra. Repetition is a very effective way to influence your attitude; so, feel free to tell yourself "I'm really enjoying this task, I'm really enjoying this task, I'm really enjoying this task." Even if you repeat this to yourself on the superficial level, you'll begin to view the task differently. Any comment or thought repeated often enough becomes ingrained in your subconscious mind and soon begins to direct your thinking and actions.

To be effective at managing your workspace, you'll want to set some organizational goals. The goals focus your intentions and become the seeds of change in your life. Once you set clear goals, the actions you need to take will be shown to you, and your goals will begin to manifest. Clear goals produce clear results.

Don't be deceived by the simplicity of this simple affirmation technique; repetition is an effective psychological tool used by psychotherapists. As you repeat the words, they implant themselves in your subconscious mind; they become self-fulfilling. Repeatedly affirming your inherent power to achieve your desired outcome moves you toward committing to the process of organization. You can move from being "enveloped" by how little time you have to having all the time in the world. To find that easy perspective, you must slow down to the natural pace of life. Become one with the radiant, timeless nature of your being. You are complete and whole at every moment, and this is the truth of the spiritual path. In reality, you have all the time in the world.

* * *

Contemplation: Inner Power

I quiet my mind and open my heart.
I breathe in and out several times.
All is quiet and all is well.

Experience and trust the magic of beginning something new with passion and purpose. Take control over your day, and release worry and the need to control the next step. Allow yourself to be guided and led into the next best thing for you. Have faith in yourself, and by trusting your inner wisdom, the universe will make all possibilities available to you. You are strong and bold, and all is moving in the right direction to support your newfound desire.

Affirm: *I trust the next step that is laid down before me, as I know it is guiding me into a great next possibility. I'm blessed for this wisdom and the strength it gives me. I am complete within myself and know that my mind is opening to a well-balanced and organized existence. Now that I choose an attitude of gratitude for all that I have and experience, I'm powerful beyond measure and can succeed at organizing my life.*

•••
THE GIFTS YOU BRING

Life is a journey. It is not a race.
Do yourself a favor and slow down.
—RICHARD SWENSON

The gifts you bring to the world are especially pronounced in the workplace. This is a place where your talents have the chance to shine. Why not bring the best of yourself to where you work? I once had a supervisor who said as she walked through the door, "Good morning, Sunshine!" It was such a nice way to start the day. Everyone's experience of his or her day can be enhanced by you! A vibrant, positive energy disseminates when you are able to share your highest and best self in the workplace.

You can contribute to the feeling of appreciation and purpose in your workplace by staying attuned to your highest self throughout your day. If you're not anxious inside, you can gracefully accept things as they are, and this calm approach to the world spreads to everyone around you. By being mindful of your spiritual essence and staying attentive to the present moment, you inspire your coworkers to do the same, even if they have no awareness of your practice. When you're in synchronization with the sacred, with the flow of life, you enter a different dimension of awareness that is focused, nonreactive, and hence, productive. Everyone in your work environment will appreciate being better able to experience his or her days as timeless, calm, and grounded.

If you can create a vision of neatness and simplicity and bring that vision with you to your workplace, you'll be surprised at how infectious it is. If, for example, you make a point of cleaning up after yourself in your office kitchen, chances are the next person in there will clean up after himself too. By keeping a tidy, clean space, you're letting everyone around you know that you respect and value them—in turn, they're encouraged to reciprocate those qualities.

You bring your talents, your calmness, and your sense of order to the workplace, but the most important gift that you give is the gift of yourself. That gift is so precious and valuable, acknowledge that by allowing your most thoughtful, purposeful, and compassionate you to show up everywhere you go. The limitations of your past need not be carried into your future. Nothing is too good to be true; nothing is too much to ask of the universe's guiding force of good. This force is the silent power behind all things that you see in your physical world, and you are responsible for using it to make your good, and that of others, come to light. Your creativity shines at work when you connect to the source of your creation and stay open to whatever lies ahead.

* * *

Contemplation: Open

I quiet my mind and open my heart.
I breathe in and out several times.
All is quiet and all is well.

You have space all around you when you feel calm and comfortable in your environment; it lets you connect more closely to your center, the core of your being. Because your mind is in order, your space and time are also in order and allow for a larger expression of what is possible. By giving up control, you remain open to whatever the universe will bring to you, knowing that it is for your greatest good.

Affirm: *Paying attention to any areas of divine discontent, I open up to a greater reality and step out into the life that is waiting for me. I sense there is more to this experience, and by keeping my life in order, I'm able to explore my deeper self and uncover what is there. I am empowered by divine strength. I am connected with the sacred in me.*

• • •

Happiness and peace come from creating order in your home and workplace. How free and light you will feel when you've started to envision spaces that are tidy and organized, where there is a place for everything and everything is in its place. An organized space provides an environment in which you can hear your inner voice and let your gifts blossom. Now, let's look at the sacredness of your life and the joy that awaits you.

PART V

YOUR SACRED LIFE

The sacred rights of mankind are not to be rummaged for among old parchments or musty records. They are written, as with a sunbeam, in the whole volume of human nature, by the hand of the divinity itself; and can never be erased or obscured by mortal power.
—ALEXANDER HAMILTON

Understanding that your life is sacred and that your experiences are holy and divinely created is a serious self-revelation. When you begin to cherish yourself and not see your life as a dress rehearsal, things shift. When your kindness toward yourself grows, you will also feel more forgiving and loving of others. No matter what came before, you are under God's grace no matter what. When you say, "I forgive myself," or "I'm sorry. Please forgive me," something happens. By saying "I'm sorry," you don't need God's forgiveness. But rather you're asking God to give you strength so you can forgive yourself.

You can move mountains when you embrace your divine heritage and learn to love yourself and others. Honoring your time and space moves you into the creation of an amazing life. When people grow tired of continually failing at organization, they will often respond by berating themselves, blaming themselves for not being smart enough or disciplined or hard-working enough—they have no trouble deprecating themselves. (This is a flaw that is inherent to humans; everyone has this to overcome.) If, however, you can stop naming the source of your problems as paralyzing forces outside of yourself and forgive yourself for your humanness, you can be free. You can have a comforting, orderly life, honoring your innate giftedness and wisdom.

Once you forgive your past behaviors, you can open the door to bring self-compassion into the organization conversation. You must simply open your eyes to who you really are and be at peace with yourself in order to heal your surroundings. When you can accept what is and no longer judge what was, you can send forth the feeling of self-love and self-care, which will attract healing and wholeness in your life. Getting organized is just bound to happen.

How do you access your boldest self to move forward with courage when the path ahead is unknown? By holding yourself with forgiveness and compassion and by realizing the potential of your true nature. Decluttering your space begins with decluttering your mind. It is not about cleaning or tidying up but about removing or releasing something within that repeatedly attracts the same experience. Opening yourself to the power of good, abundance, and peace that is all around you is what this book is all about. This is a holy experience. Honor that and be brazen with your desires to get organized. You deserve it. The time is now. You can do it.

Most things in this world tend to push you toward attachment and away from connecting to your sacredness. In the process of following those thoughts, you lose the wisdom of your higher truth. That which truly sustains you and gives you life becomes distant and murky. Enveloped in meeting your daily needs and managing your to-do list, masking your neuroses and fears with entertainment, your mind rebels against the revelation of your deepest truths. It takes a good deal of practice to reveal to yourself the clear open field that is a peaceful mind. Yes, any time is the right time to begin, even a time of crisis. When I'm working through this process and concerned that I will never get organized, I have to write things down, get them out of my head to really see what is there.

a) Write down one thing that troubles you about getting organized *(Example: Don't know where to begin.)*

b) Write down how you are feeling. *(Example: I am feeling depressed and stuck.)*

c) Allow yourself to move through those feelings. What would be the exact opposite of that feeling? Write down the flipside of that feeling. *(Example: I am energized and inspired.)*

d) What are you going to do next? *(Example: I am going to organize my papers on the kitchen counter.)*

e) Reward yourself.

Once you have this subtle shift in your consciousness, the space around you will change and the disorganization will leave you. You won't need to keep attracting the same experiences. If you can hold the thought that the greater good is yet to unfold, then it will in the right time. Hold the possibility of having an organized life in your mind. My wish is for you to focus your life on having experiences and memorable moments, not filling your space with never-ending material objects and your time with meaningless distractions from the magnificence that you really are.

You were born to live the life that you envision. Why not spend your time connecting to your talents and to the people you love? Why not give gifts that you make, such as baked and knitted items, or some flowers from your garden? I urge you to develop a mindful consuming practice, where you slow down, determine what you need, and buy only that, and start valuing quality of your life over the quality (and quantity!) of your things. When the major issues are healed and there is peace in your mind, your heart, and your space, you can get into the flow of your life and release your true potential. Be present, do one thing at a time, and stop multitasking (which gives you a false sense of achievement), and you will undoubtedly bring more peace to your life.

Chapter Thirteen
FORGIVENESS

True forgiveness is when you can say,
"Thank you for that experience."
—Oprah Winfrey

It is so refreshing to let go of the stories of one's past and the emotions that are carried in connection with them. The personal work you do to improve yourself and live the life that you know is possible pays off when you open yourself to good experiences by forgiving yourself and letting go. There is an organizing seed within you right now that is turning to the sun, finding the strength to grow and embracing a life with a lot less chaos.

Forgiving oneself is a huge component of moving this ball forward. When you are able to mend the mind and the heart, you will make your life better by honoring yourself and feeling empowered to move into the direction of your dreams, now. When you deny the present moment, you suffer because forgiveness begins in the present. In the now, you can envision what is possible, what makes you feel good, and be moved toward a better organized life. Saying to yourself, "An organized life is possible," rather than, "I was never successful at getting things organized, why should I even try?" is what changes things. You don't need to actually know the "five steps to an organized life," but be open to move in that direction. Be in an organized place consciously, and it will eventually appear in your life. Failing to forgive the past, yourself, others, or anything that prevented you from attaining what you thought you wanted (or thought you deserved) no longer serves you.

The present moment is the only moment in which you can heal. God's presence works through you to forgive yourself and to heal others. You live in light, love and possibility. However, fighting the present moment by staying continually busy and active and distracted, is the habit for most of us. Becoming overwhelmed by your responsibilities doesn't make you a more valuable parent, child, spouse, employee, boss, or citizen of the planet. Doing more than you can effectively do and constantly feeling anxious about something that needs to be done, gives you very little time to deal with your inner fears and to be calm and present with what is really going on.

If you find it impossible to claim responsibility for who you are and for the situation in which you find yourself, you are undoubtedly fixated on the past. You aren't your history; dwelling in yesterday will not help. It is greatly empowering to free yourself from the past and to give yourself space in the present to forge a path that is just for you. Forgive yourself, and where there is suffering or pain, investigate it. Don't turn away; turn within. Look at the pain, greet it and you will eventually one day be at peace with it. (This takes work and time.)

...

RESPONSIBILITY

One does not become enlightened by imagining figures of light,
but by making the darkness conscious.
—CARL JUNG

When you own your experience, and by that I mean take responsibility for what has happened to you and what can happen, you are empowered. Taking responsibility for yourself can rejuvenate your strength when tackling deep organizational issues. Being responsible might begin with how you relate to time. Good time management releases stress, combats anxiety, and allows you to have some quality of life. Find your inner rhythm. When is the best time for you to be productive? When is a good time to rest and refresh? No one is at his or her best all the time. Amen!

Always check in to see how you are really feeling. There is always a time to relax and feel okay about getting off the treadmill of life and all the demands that are placed upon you. When you're in constant motion, it becomes hard to separate irrelevant information from important information; it becomes more difficult to unwind. If you can pause and become calm and turn the switch off, you can figure out the next right steps. You are able to solve your organizing problems and take responsibility for the quality of life you have.

You want to claim a clean slate in this moment and affirm the truth of what is possible—that you can get organized. A lot of the constant motion that you require of yourself is a way to avoid the discomfort of the present. You're better at staying stuck in the past, blaming other people or circumstances for whatever isn't going "right" in your life. If you're like many people, you continue to hold on to old habits and unpleasant memories because that is what feels easy, comfortable, and right. When you're full of resentment, anger, and regret, you don't have any room for love and self-acceptance.

But personal power and freedom arise from taking responsibility for your past and forgiving all those involved. You realize that the attention you gave to yourself as the victim of a situation was misplaced, and with your attention on the here and now, you can experience the power of the infinite presence of peace, beauty, and order. You're no longer held back by your past; everyone has made mistakes or done things that they regret.

Do you feel like time is your nemesis? The perceived lack of time is typically a root cause of an organizing disorder in many people's lives. Owning your past actually gives you more time because you don't need to waste another moment rehashing events or wrongs in your mind. You're free to center within yourself, focus your attention, and devote your newly-found mental space to the creativity of getting organized. You can solve any problem. Believe in yourself, and see what takes shape.

. . .

Contemplation: Powerful Beyond Measure

I quiet my mind and open my heart.
I breathe in and out several times.
All is quiet and all is well.

Forgiveness is your choice, freeing you from the pain of the past. Today is a bright, shiny new day in a life that is definitely good. Be proud of yourself for holding your belief that you can get the job done. You are the only one that can make yourself feel really good about yourself. You are the one that is talking to you every second of the day. Feel great that you are moving toward something that you have always wanted to do, knowing it is giving you a great return on your investment. You can do anything, just do it!

Affirm: *I forgive myself for what has been negative self-talk about my ability to get organized. I take responsibility for my life, letting go of thoughts that no longer serve my new sense of self. I let go of blaming others for my clutter and lack of order. I am responsible for my organized life, am able to do the work that needs to be done, and am grateful that I know this. I forgive myself and all others who may have hurt or wronged me, and I move on in a loving and dignified way. I am a wise and loving and creative person. My confidence increases as I see myself clearly and know what I am capable of in my life. I am a shining expression of the Spirit. My schedule is reasonable and unhurried. My home is comfortable, peaceful and beautiful.*

. . .
HEALING

The art of healing comes from nature, not from the physician.
Therefore the physician must start from nature, with an open mind.
—PARACELSUS

Many people get upset with themselves and feel badly about the situation they're in during the transition of moving from disorganized to organized. They stop loving who they are and fail to remember what is possible in the future. The world of shame and anxiety, fear and embarrassment is always close at hand when you are getting organized. Living in judgment of yourself and being critical that you can't keep it together, you release negative energy into the space that unfortunately needs it the least.

Spiritual practices take commitment. Living a life that is organized and easy to maintain takes dedication to your organizing practice. When you realign and want to heal what is, you must commune with the higher self that allows you to surrender and trust that the good is moving in the right direction. Whenever I feel overwhelmed by my current situation, I have to believe that whatever I am experiencing is the most helpful for the evolution of my consciousness. The truth of you is wholeness and perfection, and you're renewed each moment as you abide in that awareness. You are never bound by the past. The universe never withholds good from you. Freedom, peace, and happiness are always yours to accept. A bad experience shouldn't be the script that you read from as you create tomorrow.

Choosing forgiveness offers true healing and freedom from the pain of the past. Loving is the highest vibration of God's healing presence. You are in this self examination phase of organization and it is good. Whatever happened before is done and provides direction for your next organizing action steps. You are shifting your experience, healing is already taking place.

* * *

Contemplation: Free of the Past

I quiet my mind and open my heart.
I breathe in and out several times.
All is quiet and all is well.

Nothing from the past ever truly blocks the divine flow of good to you. Your source is all loving, all giving; it knows neither lack nor limitation, neither fault nor shortcoming. If you've allowed a belief that life is working against you to block your good or keep you trapped in limitation, you may now release that belief. As you stay attuned to the divine presence within, you find a new freedom. Therefore, stay and renew your commitment to your spiritual growth, freeing yourself up from past stories and moving through the many different emotions of forgiveness. Stay focused first on God.

Affirm: *Today the past is wiped clean. There is only freedom and renewal. I move forward with a trusting openness to the flow of good in my life, and I am grateful. Choosing forgiveness offers true healing and freedom from the pain of the past. Keeping the current of love open and free, I hold on to joy and let the right people, solutions, and ideas enter my life while organizing. Forgiveness is my choice, freeing me from the pain of the past. I am open and ready to receive.*

CHAPTER FOURTEEN
COMPASSION

You yourself, as much as anybody in the entire universe,
deserves your love and affection.
—GAUTAMA BUDDHA

Rather than dreading getting organized and exaggerating the effort and skill it takes to get it done, you should focus on the possibility of what could be and cultivate self-compassion for the organizing journey you're on. Rather than anticipating the worst outcome, why not expect the best? Your organizing undertaking may feel daunting, and even overwhelming, but don't forget that you're living under the grace of God—forgiven, supported, and loved. You are washed with the divine essence of love and kindness, and you can move forward knowing that every difficult situation that you encounter must be there for you to grow and learn from.

By labeling yourself as disorganized, you add another "layer" to your organizing tasks. But you mustn't take your thoughts so seriously—you can change them. You can change your ideas about yourself, what is possible, and what being organized looks like in your life. Who said that everything is black and white? You needn't live in the absolute, believing that "Once this has happened, it will happen again," or "I've never been able to keep anything straight." Ideas like these feed you lies about your own capability and worthiness.

I know the strange pull that such ideas exert on people, even though such negativity robs them of the joy they so deserve. You want instead to create a mental picture containing a future of possibilities and self-love. Do you have compassion for others when they're struggling or blue? Why would you not offer yourself that same compassion? Like the forgiveness I spoke of earlier, offer yourself the same type of compassion that you would provide someone else who has a pattern of negative beliefs about themselves.

Nearly all the people I meet feel that they have hectic, sometimes chaotic schedules filled with responsibilities and obligations, with rarely enough time to accomplish all they have to do. It seems counterintuitive, but by making time for personal nurturing, solitude, and reflection, you will gain more strength and stamina in your daily life. Giving yourself permission to lie down on the grass and look up at the sky, feeling your connection with the higher consciousness and remembering that you're perfect just the way you are will ease your mind and calm your soul. Recognizing the wonderful self that you are, and freely offering that self the unreserved compassion that you would offer someone else, will go far in giving you the energy to be effective in both your day-to-day activities and in your organizing efforts (which, with practice, will become one and the same).

You must never forget that you are God's representative. As an expression of the divine, why would you not honor your own sacredness? Why would you not commit to being your best self? Commit to a spiritual practice, to accepting what is and discovering what is separating you from loving yourself. Commit to loving yourself, so that no person or thing can prevent you from living from that place of beauty, joy, and empowerment. Commit to compassion.

An awareness of your dignity and value is critical for you to experience wisdom and joy. By feeling gratitude for what you have and by using your gifts in service to God and others, your riches will increase. You must know that your life is in order and allow in the calm and joy that this knowledge brings, keeping your mind on the good that surrounds you. You need never overreact to circumstances or let them move you away from your center. When I set out to accomplish something, I tell myself to focus on the task at hand, what is mine to do, and during it all, I hold myself with love and support, as a mother holds her child. Go ahead and try it; give yourself the luxury of just focusing on one thing at a time.

You can heal whatever injuries you're carrying and whatever new disturbances come your way. Whatever appears in your life, no matter what it is, it need not shake you because you dwell in a space of self-respect and self-love. Metaphysicians assume that if you can feel it, you can heal it. If you see a behavior or a fear about organizing and it bothers you, then this awareness is there for a healing. You may have no idea why you are disturbed by a particular organizing dilemma or experience or feeling in your life, and it may not really matter. Once you have the conscious awareness that something is an issue for you, you can look it in the eye and let it go.

• • •

LOVE

In order to carry a positive action,
we must develop here a positive vision.
—DALAI LAMA

I believe that every spiritual journey is what American spiritual teacher Marianne Williamson calls a "return to love." Love truly is the response to fear, confusion, and disorder. Stand in the flow of love that is all around you, under the grace of God, where your destiny becomes clear. Living as your best self, rooted in your integrity, forgiveness, and compassion, you're bound to taste the fruit of your efforts. When I center my thoughts on what I want most in my life, self-love is guiding me in that discovery. The silence is where discoveries are made and where you find comfort and serenity.

Spiritual practice takes commitment. You may be challenged by attempts to find the spiritual truth lurking within something you deem a negative experience. I promise you, there is a lesson for you there somewhere, and yes, it may be a bit of work to accept it. But the benefit is incalculable. Do you want to live a life of peace, joy, and abundance? Such a life takes dedication to your practice. It's that consistent Holy Communion with your higher self that allows you to let go, surrender, and trust that your good is at hand. Loving yourself is the greatest way to uplift yourself.

In keeping with the idea of self-love, you can organize from a loving perspective. Why not begin with your home, the space that has the greatest impact on your day? Your home exists for you to find rest and refuge from a busy world that always wants your attention. You want to create spaces in your life where your inner needs are nurtured and your higher ideals become more apparent. In your space, release rather than acquire, and you will be better able to see your purpose and allow your abilities to shine. Find that connection and affinity with your space, and be aware of it.

At a deeper level, cleaning out your space can be seen as moving out the stagnant energy of your life, creating space for something new and special to come in. So, if you want more inner peace, take the time to establish outer peace. Be critical (yet kind to yourself) in determining what you are surrounding yourself with. When I move in the energy of self-love, I can claim a clean slate and affirm the truth. My confidence increases as I see myself clearly. I feel like I can do almost anything, as I know I will be successful and triumphant. Divine love is all encompassing and is, in fact, the essence of your being. As you relax and simply be yourself, you are revitalized. As you bask in the stillness, you experience your eternal oneness with the infinite love and peace of the divine.

You can live from your memories or from your inspiration. The former are old programs. But the latter is a message from the divine. And the only way to hear the divine and receive inspiration is to make room in your mind. Forgive, love yourself, and throw away memories of suffering or unhappiness. Allow the divine to find its way into your being. As Isaiah 30:15 states, "In returning and rest you shall be saved; in quietness and in trust shall be your strength."

∘ ∘ ∘

Contemplation: Self-Love

I quiet my mind and open my heart.
I breathe in and out several times.
All is quiet and all is well.

Commit to being the best that you can be, loving yourself through this process of organization and decluttering. Commit to this aspect of your spiritual practice, surrendering to the process and returning to self-love whenever the need arises. You are wise, loving, and free. Restore your well-being by taking time to do nothing. Let go of worry, and embrace the love of God. Release any belief that you have to do more or become someone better to be worthy of God's acceptance and love. Be compassionate to yourself and to others throughout this organizing experience. Commit to love.

Affirm: *In every challenging situation, I rely on the guidance of my inner wisdom. Mistakes are tools for my growth. I learn from each one and am wiser for it. I pick myself up and keep moving ahead. I love who I am as I move through the organizing process, walking on my spiritual path with courage and confidence. I connect with the sacred within. I am empowered by divine strength.*

• • •

MEDITATION

Meditation is simply about being yourself and knowing something about who that is. It is about coming to realize that you are on a path whether you like it or not. Namely the path that is your life.
—Jon Kabat-Zinn

Meditation, consciously letting go of relative time and entering absolute time, is a profound tool for self-awareness and self-understanding. When you're calm enough to quietly look within, you can see your past painful emotions, impatience, and unmet aspirations without judgment. Meditation develops your ability to see the sources of your emotions and thoughts, and shines a loving light on why you might hoard, why you might constantly shop, why you might feel exhausted by all the duties of life.

The addiction of the decade is the one I call "always doing something." This addiction is an advanced form of laziness. It keeps us busily occupied with tasks so we don't have to face the truth. In response to my personal experience of this addiction, my strategy is to try to do the right thing rather than a lot of things. Like everyone, I'm seeking a life that fills me with joy. I know that the foundation of that life is living from the perfection that resides within me, instead of being engaged in incessant outer distractions.

Yes, being productive is important—even necessary—to my life. Yet constant doing can damage my health, and will most certainly keep me from knowing my intrinsic value and experiencing love. Try sitting still for just two minutes—set the timer on your oven or phone. Allow yourself to enjoy doing nothing, and you will feel more filled up with the right stuff, the everlasting peace and love that everyone seeks. Mindfulness expert Jon Kabat-Zinn said, "Meditation is the only intentional, systematic human activity which at bottom is about *not* trying to improve yourself or get anywhere else, but simply to realize where you already are."

A daily meditation practice is a commitment to spiritual growth, and I believe it's a surefire way to enhance your sense of well-being and your oneness with all things. Here is a brief lesson in meditation: sit comfortably in a chair or on the floor. (If you choose the latter, sit on the edge of a pillow, and cross your legs in front of you.) Gently place the palm of one hand into the other, with your thumbs touching each other, or place your hands on your thighs. Straighten your back. (Don't slouch against the back of the chair, and don't sit up so stiffly that you feel like you're at attention. Just keep your back comfortably straight.) Lower your eyelids so that just a bit of light is entering your eyes. Relax your jaw and mouth. Place your thoughts on your breath. Breathe naturally. Follow your breath with your mind.

If you find that you're thinking something (and you assuredly will), just allow the thought to pass and return to your breath. No matter how many times you find yourself thinking about something that is not your breath, notice the thought, and return to your breath. This is both very easy and very challenging. Don't judge the way you do it, just keep doing it. It doesn't matter how often you have to remind yourself to put away a thought and return to your breath. There is no trophy for "meditating well." Meditation is a practice, and practice makes perfect.

Meditating in this way provides a space in which you can refresh and nurture your connection to God and renew your commitment to staying centered in the Spirit. My goal in writing this book was to help you find your spiritual center in today's out-of-control, overfilled lives. You can become a master rather than a victim of relentless schedules and constant distraction and feel composed in any situation—neither rushed nor overwhelmed but peacefully in the moment. You can learn to set your own pace, a pace that makes sense in relation to who you are and what you need for your life journey to be a success.

* * *

Contemplation: One with All Life

I quiet my mind and open my heart.
I breathe in and out several times.
All is quiet and all is well.

With faith, you manifest what you imagine. Remember that good exists in the Spirit. Know that answers will come, and new perspectives will be revealed. Centered in truth, you will see beyond conflict and challenge. With a mind that is calm and full of God's presence, you can visualize everything working for your best. Because you now take the time to center in the Spirit and realize that you are responsible for your experience, obstacles rarely appear. When they do, they open a way for guidance and love to flow.

Affirm: *In every challenging organizing situation, I rely on the guidance of my inner wisdom. The light of the healing presence within me guides my way, and I am deeply connected to all that enter my experience.*

CHAPTER FIFTEEN
YOUR UNLIMITED NATURE

The present moment is filled with joy and happiness.
If you are attentive, you will see it.
—THICH NHAT HANH

A fulfilling life is yours for the asking. If you believe that there is a power in the universe that accepts your thoughts and manifests an organized life according to your beliefs, then you can become organized. When you imagine yourself getting and staying organized, staying in control of your environment and empowered by your thoughts, you open yourself to the good that is truly possible. Holmes once said, "You never saw a successful [person] who went around in an atmosphere of failure." Attitude is everything. Finding that confident place within you and operating from that knowledge, you will be better able to access the depth of who you are and what is possible in your life.

When you encourage and nurture your dreams, you find that

your life is organized, peaceful, and full of the time you need to focus on what really matters - your relationship to the Spirit. It takes time to focus on the big things, but if you are overwhelmed by simple earthly tasks, you have little opportunity to focus on the big stuff. There are unlimited possibilities to create and sustain an organized life. Just turning in that direction, that space where anything can happen, is an enormous first step.

Thoughts of order and peace must dominate your mind, and as they do, they take shape in your life. Just claiming, "I'm organized," "I have more than enough time to get this done!" will bring about a space for that thought to materialize. The first step in the renewing of the mind is desire. See what is possible. As I write this, I've been thinking about organizing my office. I have a huge desire to reshape that space, and once I can feel it and believe it, I will have it. While it is hard to accept for many people, it is ultimately for the best that they shake the chief delusion that there are causes for their less-than-satisfactory life other than their own state of consciousness. Take charge of getting organized by tapping into what your heart is telling you.

In truth, all that happens to you is a result of your state of consciousness, so you can direct your thoughts to guide you down the stream of your life. It is empowering to understand that you can change your outer world; that means that any lack of success in the past can be left behind. As Ernest Holmes once said, "If we can only experience a little good, then we shall experience but a little good." Accept the power that comes through an awareness of God, and when perplexed or struggling, turn within to feel it. You don't have to search for it; you may calmly allow the awareness of the Spirit to reveal itself to you. Don't wait; the present moment is always the most opportune in which to eliminate all negative assumptions and to concentrate only on the good. The Spirit is always listening.

There is no greater relationship than the one you have with the source from which you have come. If you tend to that relationship first and foremost, then you will find the stable footing to master other areas of your life. Your relationship with your possessions will change when you align your actions with your heart. Surrender becomes so much easier when you realize the fleeting nature of all experiences and that the only tangible thing is the here and now. I cannot overemphasize the truth that no everlasting happiness comes from the material goods that you accumulate. You will never find salvation in a new set of china.

Do not think about failing or give negativity any power in your thoughts. Go for a walk or a bike ride in the park. If you're on a break from work, see how many blocks you can walk during your break time. Find an experience that doesn't cost money, and see how you feel. You only live in this precious body for a limited time—wouldn't you prefer to spend that time cultivating wisdom and insight about who you are rather than shopping online? Wouldn't you rather spend it removing the junk from your home so you can live a beautiful, peaceful life? Your unlimited nature is yours to reveal.

The only fate governing your life is the fate determined by your own beliefs. To experience your life differently, you must hold the image of that life with all your heart. Intense burning desire combined with the intention to make good is the mainspring for action, the beginning of all successful ventures in claiming your organized, sacred life. Form a mental image, a place that gives you energy and focus. Visualize the image in your consciousness. Then feel what it's like to be in that state. Concentrate your attention on the feeling that you are already living in that space. Be still and act as if you are living an organized life. This is the path to creating your own happiness. When it comes to organizing, your unlimited nature is full of possibilities and solutions that bring about joy and peace. Something has already shifted in you. You are open to an organized life.

. . .

WILLPOWER

You illuminate or darken your life by the ideas to which you consent.
—Neville Goddard

Your organizing experience depends on your attitude to create the space in your mind and it will appear in your surroundings. Assume a different reality. You do this by imagining that you already are what you want to be and already have what you want to have. In *The Secret*, Rhonda Byrne writes, "Nothing can come into your experience unless you summon it through persistent thoughts." You are a being with the power to intervene in your experience, to change your future and get organized once and for all. As Kahil Gibran once said, "To understand the heart and mind of a person, look not at what he has already achieved, but at what he aspires to be."

Most of us are not enlightened spiritual masters. Like most people, you must work to move beyond urges to engage in excessive shopping and to cling to the things you've accumulated (no matter how little you need them). Hoarding speaks to a lack of faith that all will be provided. A more healing antidote to scarcity (of time or space) is gratitude—with gratitude comes the realization of abundance.

When you embrace the redemptive function of your imagination, you hold in your hands the solution to your problems. As Goddard claims, "If your imagination is not controlled and your attention not steadied on the feeling of the wish fulfilled, no amount of prayer or piety will produce the desire effect." As American motivational speaker Brian Tracy once said, "It doesn't matter where you are coming from. All that matters is where you're going."

Willpower is like a muscle, becoming stronger with regular use. Don't put a limit on what is possible—simply stay positive. For example, don't say "I'm just going to try to get better organized next year." Say instead, "I'm getting better organized now." When you're being positive, you don't want to limit your good and put restraints on what you can experience. Never use a time, date or monetary amount in your prayer work. Be open and allow things to enter your life and events to occur that are greater and better than you thought possible. Make your good intentions become a reality. Try this exercise:

a) Write down your intention for why you want to get organized, what that life consists of. (Get it out of your head and onto paper, so that you can really see it as something powerful).

b) Make a list of things that will benefit from better organization.

c) Affirm the truth of these benefits through prayer and affirmations. Use your willpower to keep your thoughts focused on the manifestation of the organized experience you want to have until it becomes a reality in your physical world.

* * *

Contemplation: Putting Willpower to Work

I quiet my mind and open my heart.
I breathe in and out several times.
All is quiet and all is well.

When you choose to do the will of God, you express your spiritual nature. Your willpower allows you to release what no longer serves your highest good. Focus your attention on the good you desire, and affirm your ability to accomplish what you want in life. Your will empowers your intentions and provides the fuel for their fulfillment. Using the strength of your willpower, direct the entirety of the good coming to you, and through you, to manifest. You are one with divine order. As you follow your inner guidance, you act on new ideas and change what needs to be changed. You see God as existing in everything, and you celebrate the miracle of divine order in your life. You can do it.

Affirm: *I stand in peace, knowing that I'm always guided and directed to experience my highest organized life. This peace I give to all who come into my path. I am the peace of God. In every challenging situation, I rely on the guidance of my inner wisdom. I joyously claim the gifts of a new day and am open to whatever they may be. I awaken to the precious light of a new day and to the experience of the amazing gifts awaiting me.*

· · ·

ASK AND IT WILL BE GIVEN

When you doubt your power, you give power to your doubt.
— HONORÉ DE BALZAC

Everything begins in the mind. Any idea you place in your mind becomes realized in your actual experience. When there is any form of mental clutter, such as a belief that you will fail at getting organized or that you just don't know how to do it, the creative process brings into itself an experience that is in accordance with that belief. Be brave, and demand from yourself a simpler, less stressful, more organized life. See it truly happening, as you have the power to create any kind of life you like. Do you want to be organized?

Yes, you can do it; and you will do it.

Your spiritual journey is about declaring that your life is sacred, that it is worthy of worship and understanding. Many steps along the path are filled with joy and happiness while many others may feel frightening and difficult. By releasing old agendas and trusting your inner voice, you remain open to self-discovery and receptive to new and better ideas. You are led to the highest expression of your spiritual nature—all the time. Centered in the Spirit, you remain calm and open to new insights and directions about your organizing abilities. As American metaphysician Robert Collier described it, "All power is from within and, therefore, under our control." This is where your imaginations and creativity come in. Imagination is the instrument by which you create your organized world. You're always moving toward something that wants to be expressed, and that is likely the reason you are reading this book, knowing that these words will support your next steps.

Surrender to the feeling of success, that the wish is being fulfilled. You are part of a consciousness that is alive, intelligent, and creative. All possibilities can be drawn from the universe, and in response to the law of attraction, the universe delivers select people, circumstances, and events to your life. Just ask, as you know your divine birthright, and wait for it to connect to the infinite supply that is your life.

Creativity is the medium by which the divine source speaks to you, and your use of it to unlock a beautiful and happy life path is your gift to yourself and everyone around you. Far too often, people think that this path is restricted to "real" artists, but as I mentioned earlier, everyone has the ability to use their creativity to join with their divine source in the creation of a desired outcome in their life. When you discover your creativity and express it through how you schedule your time and how you structure your space, you can start to see how important it is to be open and led by the Spirit. When you let your dreams lead and guide you, you are tapping into your creativity, and therefore, God must be nearby.

Be aware that the center of your creativity doesn't reside within your brain but within your soul. That is where inspiration and desire for connection are held and where your true, or higher, self dwells, emerging to experience the mystical and divine. Try meditating to calm your mind and allow your pure essence to come forth in the creative way that is uniquely yours. As you develop a feeling of calm, you can listen to the path that your new life will take, and it will guide your way. Your creative voice cuts through the air with direction, purpose, and joy, and releases your deepest inner wisdom.

In most cultures, creativity and spirituality are commonly manifested through music, song, and dance, and these are ways to express both the soul's desires and the joy of being. But creativity and spirituality need not be confined to traditional methods of expression; they show up in every aspect of your life, such as how you relate to and care for others, the way in which you address challenges, and the solutions you generate to better your life and the lives of those around you. Your life is your art.

The connection between your thoughts and God's thoughts are the way your creativity flourishes. Your job is to use your creativity, your ability to tap into and manifest the good of your divine source, to bring you to where you want to go next, having an organized environment in which to thrive. When you're dreaming, you are creating something from nothing and letting your higher self lead the way. While it may be a new experience for you and might feel uncomfortable at first, you must resolve to support yourself in your new vision, always staying the course and seeking answers from within.

Within each and every one of us exists openness to the infinite of all life. Small steps lead to big triumphs. Every day is a new beginning in which infinite possibilities present themselves. You know you've let yourself step away from the flow, when you begin to feel like you're not getting enough done or you're stressed about the day ahead. In contrast, when you surrender to the knowledge that all is truly well, time seems to stretch for you, allowing you to accomplish what you need to, in comfort. Your experience improves, markedly.

If you grew up in a cluttered environment or you've always been late or frazzled, you can begin to live in a conscious way. As you change your thinking, you change your relationship to time and space. You have the power to make this shift and to move toward your joy. Living in humility, your understanding that you exist under God's grace, allows your wisdom to shine. When I find organizing patterns in my life that I want to improve and reinforce, I open myself to the Spirit's guidance, insight, and blessings. God shows me the next right action. The more gratitude I feel for the universe's boundless supply of good, the better I am able to make centered decisions, focusing on the right things to do and doing them at the right time.

You change your life by changing your attitudes and perceptions—the seeds of behavioral changes are sown when your attitudes and perceptions change toward a given subject or process. You will find that what matters more than a task's "urgency" is how you arrive at the choice to address it. When you learn that there is an opportunity to live in a new way, a host of new choices emerges. As Austrian psychiatrist and Holocaust survivor Victor Frankl said, "We have the power to choose our attitude in any given set of circumstances." Remember that. Have the courage to be brave, breathe in possibility, and allow form to arise.

You become what you think about yourself. As your perceptions and attitudes change, you begin to visualize yourself in a new role. Once your vision of yourself in the new role is clear, your thoughts and actions gravitate toward the "new" person you envision. Your mind is naturally goal-seeking. With a clear picture of your objective, you automatically move in the direction of the change or goal—and the clearer the vision of the change, the more pronounced the directed action.

You are bound to backslide on occasion; the habit of thinking defeatist thoughts is not a simple one to overcome. But whatever difficulties you may come across, remember that you are free to takes breaks and realign with your highest vision of yourself. You are always able to be present, and you are always able to love. There is nothing that is beyond your grasp. Ralph Waldo Emerson once said, "All that Adam had, all that Caesar could, you have and can do.... Build, therefore, your own world."

When you awaken to the mystery of life, you can awaken mindfulness and anchor yourself in peace and clarity. Wayne Dyer once said, "Your life is not a problem to be solved but a gift to be opened." Recognize that God works in you, through you, as you. You will become liberated from the trap of your fears, delusions, conflicts, and attachments. Your organizing difficulties and failures do not define you. Don't mistake unwanted outcomes in your past for your destiny. The peace and order you desire are already yours to have.

. . .

Contemplation: My Power to Create

I quiet my mind and open my heart.
I breathe in and out several times.
All is quiet and all is well.

Believe in your heart that what you imagine will manifest; walk in faith until it does. The love of God in you brings harmony and organization into your life. The strength of God in you provides you the will and energy to navigate any situation. Your faith gives you hope, patience, insight, and a positive frame of mind. Through the power of God in you, use your imagination to create the best organizing outcomes. You overcome any obstacles, you prevail, and you achieve your dreams.

Pause before the blank canvas of your life until you feel guided to create. Once inspired to move in a particular direction, your creativity comes alive and you begin your masterpiece, each movement carefully selected with the master creator's direction. I delight in the fresh start that Spirit gives me to start organizing. You are eternal energy and are one with the world. As Goddard claims, "In the midst of what appear to be contradictions in your life, there is only one principle at work, only your consciousness operating." The stillness is where God protects and enfolds you with warmth and healing. From physical comfort to feeling loved, God ensures all your needs are fully meet. You are whole, protected, and complete. Have faith in the power of your thoughts.

Affirm: *In every challenging situation, I rely on the guidance of my inner wisdom. I am God in action. I no longer focus my attention on undesirable circumstances in my life. Instead, I put my attention on the goodness of God, knowing that God's will is always available to me. Goodness brings happiness, and I now embrace heartfelt happiness in all areas of my life. I am organized and in great peace.*

Concluding Thoughts

Your life is sacred. This knowledge can move you in the right direction, to a much greater experience of awakening, if you are conscious about how you live. Knowing now that nothing comes into your space without you opening the door for it, you are free to move from your past thoughts about how challenging organizing can be, to a new place where you welcome the insights and guidance that will ultimately help you to achieve organization. Any form of interruption or disconnect from source, like living a chaotic life, should be a wake-up call that inspires change and awareness. When something unpleasant is present in your life, ask yourself "What am I mentally creating in order for this to happen?", "What are my thoughts about organizing?", and "Where do they come from?". Pause, inquire within.

You have learned that the first thing you have to do to get organized is to change your attitude toward and perceptions about it. By starting with a compassionate heart that desires an organized and peaceful life, and by subsequently emitting feelings that reflect the achievement of that desire, your life will shift in that direction. You have to put your thoughts beyond what is in order to attract something that is desirable. Initially, you don't create through action, you create by directing your mental energy, and that calls forth actions and experiences that support the outcome that you desire. You don't create new organizing situations through action and doing initially. But rather, you create a new organizing possibility through your energetic thoughts about it.

Remember that if you want to erase clutter from your life, begin by having thoughts of abundance, of fullness in the present moment. If you are feeling anxious or continually stressed out or completely overwhelmed, this is your indicator that you are denying yourself access to all manner of cooperation from the universe, demonstrated through people, ideas and joy. You organize what you prioritize, so don't prioritize being busy rather be that peace, tap into that peace all around you. Don't panic. When you feel really overwhelmed, stop, breathe, and bring in the light of Spirit.

The fastest way to improve any situation is to make peace with your current circumstances. One of the many life-lingering objectives is to be at peace with where you are – allowing nothing to take you away from that center of stillness, clarity, insight and joy. Also, creating a physical and mental space to rest between the actions of life and the busyness of work, will bring about a healthier quality of life. By making lists of the most positive aspects you can recognize about your current situation, you bring yourself into deeper alignment by asking yourself, "Am I living in harmony with my desires?" and "Do my place, my schedule and my thoughts create the quality of life that I know is truly possible?"

You will desire to have fewer things and will experience the extra energy to tackle the projects that you have put off. I find that turning to nature, going on a hike or to the park, really sustains and fulfills me more than anything else I can do. Remember that less is always more. Some people think they will finally be fulfilled when they obtain all the things they desire. But, if you don't feel good on your way to that magical place, it will always be out of reach. You have to be satisfied with what is while you're reaching for more.

As this vision becomes part of your psychological makeup, you see yourself in this new role constantly throughout the day, and your thoughts and actions gravitate toward this newly organized life. Your mind loves to set goals, and with clear intentions and a big desire, you can have the organized life that you've only dreamed of. It is already happening. Seek out a living space or a job where there is an energetic connection to your joy and happiness. Again, begin by asking, "How much of my day do I spend in deep connection to my goals and desires?"

Being calm enough to gauge your current inner discussion about organization as this will propel you along the path of living a clutter-free life. By understanding that "this time around" is very sacred and meaningful, you begin to shift your perceptions, and your environment takes shape in support of that. Play the "flip it" game as much as possible, reciting positive expressions alongside the next action steps, and say your prayers! Keep your desire alive, and see how your life transforms. Hard work isn't the main path to well-being – feeling good is.

There is something that everyone on this planet yearns for, and that is a deeper connection to their divinity, their sacredness. My life grows richer as I invest my time and attention in contemplation. Simple living is achieved by acknowledging that all life flows from one source – God. The bar of success in life isn't how much you have but rather the love that is in your heart. The "simple, bare necessities" of life do not carry a price tag. Simple pleasures, like hiking or being with friends, allow you to easily recognize that God's presence is at the center of all joy.

When you give yourself the power to use your thoughts to make better choices and to actively visualize the life that you desire, knowing that you are supported and loved, then organizing success awaits. When you understand that consciousness is the true North Star that guides you in the right direction, and trust in your own divine truth, you shall move into the realm where organizing is a success. By creating organizational flow among your surroundings, the eternal moment is felt, and you become present and use spiritual time management principles to improve your life at home and at work. Visualize order. Live in order. Live in peace.

APPENDIX

AFFIRMATIONS

- Positive thinking not only creates positive results, but it also combats mental chatter.

- Being positive allows the mind to envision positive solutions and shift our attitudes and thus, experiences.

- Start each day by affirming your organizational success, whatever that may be.

- "Flip-It." When doubt appears about you being on time, or organizing your photos etc., "I'm always late," or "I can't do this!" say the exact opposite. ("I'm on time today!" or "I can get this done!") Say this until you believe it. Let it register in your consciousness. Feel it.

- An affirmation should be:
  - Positive
  - In the present time – now!
  - "I..." or "My..."
  - Not too long – easy to remember
  - Repeated many times a day, until you see it demonstrated in your life.

- I also encourage you to keep them in strategic place in your home. (Bathroom mirror, refrigerator, computer monitor etc. Some place where you spend a little extra time, repeatedly throughout the day.)

- I also like to encourage you to write the down and carry them with you in your purse, handbag, etc. I like to keep mine in my wallet and always look at it throughout the day. When I feel complete with it, I discard it and create a new one.

- The more you use your affirmations, your life will start to reflect them.

- Following, there are three sections, beliefs, time, and clutter, with 15 affirmations in each. Either focus on your area of concern and read all those affirmations, or find one or two and repeat them. Write your own in the space provided.

Affirmations: _____

_____

_____

ORGANIZING BELIEFS

- I am getting organized now.
- I have all that I need.
- I am whole, complete, and perfect just as I am.
- I clear the chaos from my mind/heart, I can clear the chaos from my life.
- I gladly release the items that I've had for years and welcome other forms of fulfillment to become part of my life.
- I am experiencing a sense of peace in my life and am learning to create peace in my organizing solutions.
- I choose thoughts and words that support my organizational changes.
- I've made peace with the past and embrace my organized life.
- I enjoy creating order around me.
- I commit to change and welcome a new way of being organized.
- I listen to my heart and am lead to setting priorities.
- I consume less and feel great.
- I always find what I'm looking for.
- I'm grateful for creating such organized spaces.
- I embrace this newly organized life.

Affirmations: _____

_____

_____

TIME

- There is plenty of time for me to get organized.
- I'm mindful as to what I am doing,
- I have more than enough time to get everything done.
- I am always in the right place, doing the right thing, at the right time.
- I am using my time wisely and intelligently.
- I am conscious of how I spend my time.
- I have more free time because I'm now organized.
- Time is my friend.
- Conscious time management comes natural to me.
- I take time to manage my schedule and consciously create my life.
- Simplifying takes time.
- I manage my time with productive and ease.
- I am always doing the right thing at the right time.
- I am consciously doing…
- I'm productive and at peace.

Affirmations: _____

_____

_____

_____

CLUTTER

- I am good at putting things away when I am done with them.
- No job is too hard. I see beyond my chaos.
- My space is uplifting and I have everything I need.
- I am very discriminate with things I bring into my life.
- I purchase items that make a positive difference in my life.
- I am purging with ease and understanding.
- I forgive myself and release any thoughts of judgment.
- I shop with purpose and intention.
- I have all that I need. Do I need it or want it?
- I release what doesn't serve me.
- Simplifying brings me great joy.
- I stay focused when I'm purging.
- I live in the present – an organized life.
- I'm grateful for order.
- I'm a perfect expression of God in action.

Affirmations: _____

_____

_____

_____

PRAYERS

When you experience a moment of doubt about the prospects of having an organized life, a calm and peaceful life in your space, come to this section and find the topic that most resonates with you at that moment. Just sit with the prayer that you need, and repeat it to yourself until you feel a shift come over you and a change happening. The life-affirming prayers below will help you readjust to what is possible and not repeatedly mull over what didn't happen or what can't be. Setting your mind to the right heartfelt intention will greatly assist in turning your situation around. You can heal yourself and your circumstances.

During this moment of centering and setting a thoughtful intention, you're likely to also have a perception of the Holy Presence that runs through all life. As you shift the attitude from what is happening now to what is possible, you're reminded that the infinite source of all that you desire is within you. For the prayers below to be most impactful, they should be read and repeated with a certain mind-set.

First, center yourself in an awareness of the abundance and good that is in your life (even if it is ever so small). Second, acknowledge that there is only one—one life, one truth, one source. Third, realize that it dwells within you. Fourth, powerfully claim this new experience of having, rather than longing for, your desire. Fifth, express gratitude for the good things in your life. Finally, trust that the best is yet to come.

Find an area in your home (any quiet corner or room is fine) in which you can stop, think, and observe what you're experiencing. Let go of judgment and the need for perfection, and find a place to rejuvenate your entire being and align your mind with your greater good.

. . .

ACCEPTANCE

I know that as I move in the direction of healing my life, there is one source, one power that exists, has existed, and will forever exist. Everything in my experience confirms and accepts it as my truth. The Spirit of wholeness, love, and peace are in my consciousness, in my being, and in all that I do. So, I accept what is, what has been, and what will be as I radiate peace and a positive attitude in all that I undertake, particularly in organizing my home, my office, and my life. I sense a power within me that allows for a greater good to exist. So, I accept this as my truth and know that the best is yet to come. As I focus on my being, rather than my doing, I get more of the right things done. All is well. I'm at peace in this moment. Amen.

* * *

ATTRACTION

How good it is to know that there is nothing that I have to do but align my thoughts of what I think is possible. In my mind, I am open and receptive to the sacred energy that has created everything I see. This energy exists within me, creating new divine expressions. This inner wisdom and activity of God underlies everything I do. I attract what I focus on into my life. I know that the divine right action is happening in my life and that it is bringing me into greater harmony with my surroundings, how I relate to time and how I feel at the end of the day. I call it forth into the reality of infinite possibilities and infinite solutions to my organizational concerns. I am powerful, and the harmony that I'm sending out returns to me. And as I call it forth, the Spirit expresses itself in its own unique, divine way. As I stand in this space, I am grateful for what I can achieve just using my mind to align and guide me toward my greater good. The Spirit leads the way. Amen.

* * *

COMPASSION

There is a presence and power in the universe right now, the presence of love, joy, kindness, and grace, that is available now. My relationship with the divine is a relationship of love, and that love washes over me as I move throughout my day. I let go of self-critical thoughts and embrace the love and respect of this energetic flow that is always at my command. I open to my magnificence, my radiance, and my divine center to pour forth love from an open heart outwardly to others and inwardly to myself. When I struggle in difficult times, I release myself from worry and judgment and embrace the freedom and peace that is mine. These divine creative impulses uplift me and return me to love and adoration. I'm thankful for a way to find that peace that is meant for me and to see the holy, the sacred, and the beautiful in this radiant new beginning. I release these intentions, let them rise up to the sky, and feel in my body the good that is coming into my space and life. Amen.

* * *

CREATIVITY

The oneness of all life is omnipresent, always and forever. That oneness exists in all forms and is constantly changing and moving into a greater and fuller expression of God. So, I recognize the present evolution of consciousness as the only thing happening. I'm one with the multitude of divine ideas and creativity, as I am never separate from God. I have never been separate as I turn to God and speak a word of absolute creativity as my life. With every word I speak, the organizing path is coming into greater clarity before me. I express myself in a way that releases my inner truth, knowing that I'm always moving in the direction of the greater, fuller, and richer expression of the divine. I'm grateful that I was put forth as a seed of God holding the essence of a unique self-expression. Amen.

* * *

EMOTIONS

Slowing down to feel the presence within, the wholeness, the completeness, and the fullness that God is, I relax into my center, knowing that oneness is all there truly is. I profoundly know and deeply feel this presence expressed within me each and every single day. Whatever yearnings I feel within, I allow them to arise and notice them for what they are. I develop a relationship with my feelings, acknowledging whatever comes up, even worries about tomorrow that take me out of being present to what is happening today. I open myself up to this awareness, allowing feelings to come forth in a loving and gentle attitude. I just bless and give thanks for this day, letting it be as it is, and I am at peace in the midst of this experience. In gratitude, I am aware of my emotions and am grateful that I have the ability to transcend them. I am grateful to be centered in this One that it is working through me. I let it be, and so it is. Amen

* * *

FAITH

I have faith in the infinite nature of the Spirit, the grand architect of life, the compassionate and gentle maker of us all. There is one presence in my life. God is in all; God is good, omnipotent, and all-loving. The moon, the stars, the fruit, and the trees all come from the source of all creation. I witness this, feel this bounty, and know that the strength of all I do comes from the source of all creation. I am continually reminded of how beautiful life is. I have faith that God guides me in devising new organizing solutions that help my life. I walk in a firm belief that I will be guided until I feel the solutions that are needed to bring ease and peace into my life. I give enormous thanks for this glorious day, and my mind and actions are united under the one umbrella of the Divine. I'm deeply committed to a life that is steeped in my faith and know that I'm moved to organize and create a fresh life to the greater expression of God. I give thanks for wholeness, and I call forth peace of body, mind, and soul to move in the direction of an organized and whole life. Amen.

* * *

FORGIVENESS

What a lovely opportunity it is to turn within and to feel the presence of God right here and right now—a loving, kind energy always takes the lead, shows me mercy, and renews my hope. As I stand in this truth and anchor with the loving energy of God at work, I easily and effortlessly step into the place of wisdom and am guided by grace. I forgive myself for judging my organizational skills and know that as I move through this transition, a loving God is there to guide me in making my life the very best it can be. I remember the true teachings of God: to love ourselves, to honor ourselves, and to be generous to ourselves. As an ambassador of God, I celebrate these teachings and trust that every aspect of my being is cherished, nurtured, and filled with God's loving presence. My heart is at peace. My actions are deliberate and I face the future with wisdom, love, and strength. As I breathe and let go, I remember that this is my true being and my true nature. Forgiveness is possible all the time, and I open to and surrender into joy and possibility as I organize my life. I call forth this vision and am grateful that I know that I can be loving and forgiving to myself while I create the means to streamline my environment and my actions. Amen.

* * *

INTENTION

I acknowledge God's grace in all life, in all things, and in all activity, and this oneness lives and breathes among all creation here and now. I know that the divine justice and activity of God supports and guides me in claiming my good. As I set powerful intentions to get and stay organized, to maintain easy, low-effort systems all around me, I know that God's truth is revealing itself in my life, and there is the right unfolding of events. In all things that arise, the divine justice of God reveals itself fully and completely. There is nothing that can hinder the manifestation of my intentions; I have the support of God, and I'm grateful for this. When I accept this truth, there is always a successful outcome. Moving forward in a positive and powerful way, it's already done, and so it is. Amen.

* * *

LISTENING

I know that there is one infinite presence that dwells within all life. This presence, everywhere, in everyone, is within me as well. With this understanding, I listen to my soul. I spend time listening to the voice within as often as possible and bring it to fruition by all my actions. I listen to identify new possibilities and to see and hear the next action steps for my organizing endeavors. Joyfully accepting these new possibilities, these new discoveries, I am already experiencing organizational success. Then, I step back with an open and generous heart and listen for my next steps. Amen.

. . .

Right Livelihood

I recognize that God is all there is and all that matters. The energetic flow that creates everything, and to which everything returns, is evidence of God's power. As I am the perfection of God, right where I am, nothing needs to be changed in me. I consciously know this truth at the core of my being; I know that the Divine is unfolding right now in my life. Saying yes to the Spirit, I am called forth to my greatest expression, and the living word of God moves through my work. I know that the divine right livelihood of my being is calling me and I answer. I am fully supported in the vision I have for myself. As I allow the word to speak through me, I allow its full support to take me to my highest being. So, I give my life up to God, allow God to flow through me, to be fully activated and present to shine, uplifted by my vision. How thankful I am in knowing that which is my perfect, divine right livelihood. With grace and ease I allow this prayer to fully manifest for my highest and best good. And so it is. Amen.

. . .

Love

There is one force encompassing everything that is in existence. I know that this force is the source of all things. I know that the divine partnership that I have with my creator is manifested in all my relationships, in my love for those around me, and in my love for myself. This knowing is alive in every center of my being, in my cells, in my heartbeat, and in my breath. Total and complete self-love and encouragement are mine. As I open my heart and my mind to the surroundings of my life, examining what works and what does not,

I know that the unity that I express in my space is the unity of the Spirit that dwells within my heart. I love and appreciate myself. So, I am thankful, overflowing with love in my life. I thank the infinite wisdom for giving me my precious life so that I might experience all that is and will be. Amen.

* * *

ORGANIZATION

How generous is the Spirit, always providing the form to suit our needs. Everything is in harmony. As we become still and know that the very essence of life itself is a harmonious activity through and through, organization reigns supreme. I allow my organizational intuition to manifest, and all of my being is expressed through my orderly life. I breathe in and allow organization to express itself in every relationship and experience that is a part of my life. I surrender to the Divine and feel the love of the Divine in my body and in my mind, and I infuse all my affairs with this love. I recognize organization in every aspect of my being. I declare in this moment that order is indeed moving through me, and the energy of gratitude that nourishes and cultivates this organization in my life is in abundance now. Amen.

* * *

POSITIVITY

How good it is to recognize the breadth of the Spirit, knowing that it is everywhere and in all things. How good it is to allow the presence of the Spirit to wash over me, to know that wherever I am, and in all that I do, I am experiencing the abundance of the Spirit. How good it is to know that the generosity of the Spirit, the goodness of the Spirit, is available to me now. How fortunate I am. How good it is to breathe in the eternal breath of God, feeling that every cell within me is renewed, revitalized, and positively going forth in the best and highest direction for all. With this realization, I have a positive attitude and only attract the highest and best to come into my life. As I release old ideas that no longer serve me and I step into a higher vibration, I walk illuminated by the Spirit with positivity and joy. When I decide to get organized, I seek out what makes me happy and what is positive and alter my life to be in that flow. My life is bountiful, and I am filled with beautiful, positive energy. The highest Spirit lives within me. I am alert and aware of the Spirit as I organize. Amen.

* * *

POSSIBILITY

There is one presence, one life, one mind, and one heart. I call this presence God, and I surrender to it in this moment and know that all is well. I recognize the power of the one presence that is absolutely everywhere within the universe, and I know that this same intelligence that created all things is opening up numerous possibilities in every direction of my life. There is an infinite amount of good, abundance, beauty, and creativity, and anything that I can conceive of is capable of taking physical form. I am blessed as I go about my daily tasks—getting organized and creating systems that support the highest and best for my life. I'm in harmony with my space, and all those who come into my life are uplifted by my peace. In a small but real way, my organization helps heal the world. And I am grateful. I'm thankful. I allow it to be. Amen.

* * *

PRACTICING THE PRESENCE

There is a limitless power from which all things come. It is the thing that was here before all else. We are each derived from that power and peaceful energy. I take the peace in my heart and pass it on. When I need a healing to happen in my organizational efforts, I connect to this power and let its radiant energy bless and support my space, my calendar, and my life. I pass this energy along, blessing those with whom I come into contact, allowing me to better control my mind when I'm making decisions about what to bring into my space. I'm always grateful for God's presence and how I'm able to benefit from the wisdom of the Divine. I know that the source of all that is functions regardless of my attention but that my attitude of gratitude opens my consciousness to receiving that which is even better. So, I let it just be. Amen.

* * *

SILENCE

How good it is to come together as one and to just leave everything behind. I slow down and sit still and allow myself to be drawn into the silence. I let go of the thinking mind and the physical body and allow my breath to fall into a natural rhythm. I breathe gently, peacefully, effortlessly, allowing God's breath to flow through me. I let go of all concern about organizing, about knowing how to do it, and just slow down. I open my heart to hear what my next steps are, or to simply hear nothing, to let thoughts out but not in. I'm grateful for knowing how powerful it is to sit with myself and now trust that I will gain greater clarity and insight into how to live an organized life. I release all worry to the wisdom and the love of the universe. Amen.

. . .

TRUST

I know that there is a divine presence, a divine power and wisdom that created everything: it guides the stars, it causes the sun to shine, it lives within me and within everything that is. As I speak my word right here and right now, I call forth this divine wisdom. I activate the wisdom of the ages with my voice, and I know that my choices spring from it. I turn away from what isn't working and toward that which I seek. I ignite the law of divine action for what I choose in my life. I trust that the God who has created all things is leading me in my own divine wisdom in turning my highest desires into reality. I naturally draw wonderful experiences into my life. Thank you infinite Spirit and divine loving law of all good for already blessing me with the things that I choose. Amen.

Closing Prayer

And so this journey begins,
shifting an understanding of myself and
how I can live my life
in an organized and peaceful way.

Feeling the presence of divine order and perfection
in everything that is all around us,
I know that there is order and majestic design in all creation
and a peaceful, organized life is possible
now.

Knowing that I'm birthed in that creative source,
I'm always welcoming thoughts of possibility and
joy to lead the way in creating an organized life.
My life is peaceful and organized
now.

I breathe in thoughts of openness and success,
realizing that I have everything
within me to live an organized life.
My life is peaceful and organized
now.

I am grateful that the intelligence behind all experience
is the same intelligence that lives inside of me.
My life is peaceful and organized
now.

I set this prayer into motion,
knowing that Thy will be done
for the highest and best and for all involved.
My life is peaceful and organized
now.

My mind, time, and space, at home and at work, are in order; and
I now feel a greater sense of peace and purpose in all that I do.

Amen.